COOKIN' UP A STORM

LAURA DAKIN

SEA STORIES AND VEGAN RECIPES FROM SEA SHEPHERD'S ANTI-WHALING CAMPAIGNS

BOOK PUBLISHING COMPANY
Summertown, Tennessee

Library of Congress Cataloging-in-Publication Data

Dakin, Laura.
 Cookin' up a storm : stories and recipes from Sea Shepherd's anti-whaling
campaigns / Laura Dakin.
    pages   cm
 Includes index.
  ISBN 978-1-57067-312-2 (pbk.) — ISBN 978-1-57067-880-6 (e-book)
 1. Vegan cooking.   2. International cooking.   3. Cooking on ships.   I. Sea
Shepherd.   II. Title.
  TX837.D154 2015
  641.5'636—dc23

2014042908

Recipe photos: Warren Jefferson
Food styling: Ron Maxen and Barbara Jefferson
Cover and interior design: John Wincek

Printed on recycled paper

Book Publishing Co. is a member of Green Press Initiative. We chose to print this title on paper with
postconsumer recycled content, processed without chlorine, which saved the following natural resources:

8 trees
267 pounds of solid waste
3,996 gallons of wastewater
737 pounds of greenhouse gases
4 million BTUs of total energy

For more information, visit
greenpressinitiative.org.

Paper calculations from Environmental
Defense Paper Calculator,
edf.org/papercalculator.

Printed in The United States of America

Book Publishing Company
PO Box 99
Summertown, TN 38483
888-260-8458
bookpubco.com

ISBN 13: 978-1-57067-312-2

20 19 18 17 16 15   1 2 3 4 5 6 7 8 9

Calculations for the nutritional
analyses in this book are based on the
average number of servings listed with
the recipes and the average amount
of an ingredient if a range is called
for. Calculations are rounded up to
the nearest gram. If two options for
an ingredient are listed, the first one
is used. The analyses include oil used
for frying. Not included are optional
ingredients and serving suggestions.

CONTENTS

HUMAN	0.1 ton	6 feet
DOLPHIN	0.5 ton	10 feet
ORCA	8 tons	28 feet
MINKE	12 tons	30 feet
GRAY	35 tons	45 feet
HUMPBACK	40 tons	50 feet
SPERM	40 tons	60 feet
SEI	35 tons	60 feet
FINBACK	60 tons	80 feet
BLUE	120 tons	90 feet

INTRODUCTION

I had learned that the oceans were depleting at an alarming rate—and I was sick of feeling helpless—but I had no idea how to begin making a positive contribution. I felt upset, at a loss.

Then I met the crew of the Sea Shepherd ship, *Farley Mowat*. The captain of the *Farley* confronts killers and challenges them, never backing down, protecting the vulnerable: the legendary captain Paul Watson. A man with an impressive history of defending sea life, Captain Watson cofounded Greenpeace International in 1972 and founded the Sea Shepherd Conservation Society in 1977.

In February 2005, when I was just twenty-one, I joined Captain Watson and the crew of the *Farley Mowat* in Bermuda, and from there we set sail to defeat the barbaric harp seal killers off the east coast of Canada. I have been on many campaigns since, and during my years as a Sea Shepherd, I have learned just how screwed up the state of the oceans really is. Marine wildlife is disappearing before our eyes, and most people show little concern. The tragic case of the dying oceans is met largely with silence, like most injustices that threaten to damage cash flow to corporate kings and greedy governments.

FACTORY SHIP   8,000 TONS, 425 FEET

WHALE CHASER   1,900 TONS, 230 FEET

Veganism: Part of the Fight

The Sea Shepherd Conservation Society is a not-for-profit marine conservation organization that takes an aggressive direct-action approach to ending the slaughter of endangered and threatened marine wildlife. Sea Shepherd is not an animal rights organization; however, it is one of few environmental groups that recognizes that a vegan diet is an important weapon that can be used to fight against the ruin of the world's oceans.

I now work in the galley of the *Steve Irwin,* another ship in the Sea Shepherd fleet, and all the communal food that we prepare is vegan. A vegan diet is free of animal-based products and by-products, including fish, meat, eggs, dairy products, and honey. In addition to steering clear of foods that cause suffering, vegans avoid wearing fur, leather, and silk and using cosmetics and household cleaners that have been tested on animals or contain animal-derived ingredients. In addition, vegans don't support forms of entertainment that exploit animals, such as horse racing, bullfighting, and circuses that feature animal acts.

Sea Shepherds are unwilling to consume cows that are being fed the very sea animals we're trying to protect.

Regarding my choice to be vegan, I understand that I'm part of a privileged minority that has the luxury to make choices about food and the money to support those choices. I've also had the time to develop a relationship with food. As a human living a life with this freedom of choice, I know it's my responsibility to

extend the privilege of freedom to other lives when possible: freedom from fear, pain, injury, and disease; freedom from hunger and thirst; and freedom to express natural behaviors.

While I fight ardently for the freedom of nonhuman animals, I wouldn't describe myself as a typical animal lover: I don't want to cuddle with every cute, furry creature I see. I do, however, respect all animals—human and nonhuman alike—and acknowledge their right to exist for themselves.

Unfortunately, I am, once again, in the minority. Thousands of billions of domestic animals are slaughtered every year so that humans can get their fill of meat and dairy, can adorn themselves with leather and fur, can distract themselves with entertainment and sport, and can subject animals to scientific experimentation with dubious merit. Wild animals are under constant threat and must continue to retreat as the human population relentlessly spreads out, destroying habitat along with precious supplies of food, water, and air. It seems that to most people, animals are food, clothing, entertainment, pets, or pests; they are either wanted too much or not wanted at all.

Sea Shepherd is not an animal rights organization; however, it is one of few environmental groups that recognizes that a vegan diet is an important weapon that can be used to fight against the ruin of the world's oceans.

Vegan Ocean Warriors

Because humans have overfished the oceans so severely, Sea Shepherds believe there are no such things as sustainable fishing or aquaculture. So obviously the first thing to remove from your diet, if you want to become an ocean warrior, is any animal that is considered seafood. But the story is much bigger than that, with unnatural and unexpected factors affecting both water and land animals. And these are the factors that drive us to eat a completely vegan diet on the ships.

The first reason is bycatch. "Bycatch" is the term used to describe the animals caught during fishing that the fisher did not intend to catch. For example, a ship's crew that is bottom trawling (the ocean equivalent of clear-cutting a forest) for prawns is likely to catch unwanted tuna and sharks at the same time. Much of this bycatch is tossed back into the ocean, already dead. However, the bycatch may be kept, ground up, and sold as a cheap source of protein to be fed to land "food" animals, such as cows, pigs, and chickens. So given our understanding of this unnatural but very real scenario, Sea Shepherds are unwilling to consume cows that are being fed the very sea animals we're trying to protect. Bycatch is also sold as food for human "companion" animals, such as dogs and cats; in fact, domestic cats are the largest consumers of seafood in the world.

We also see veganism as one way to avoid compromising the food chain. For example, the oceans' smallest fish, such as sardines, are an important food source for the larger fish. However, smaller fish are increasingly targeted by the fishing industry—again, to be sold as cheap fish meal to be fed to land animals. When the

THE GOOD GUYS

population of these smaller fish, or bottom feeders, is wiped out, the oceans' ecosystems will collapse from the bottom up, with little hope of healthy regeneration.

Finally, adhering to a vegan diet is a significant individual effort toward conservation. Invasive fishing methods, such as trawling, long-lining, drift netting, and dynamiting, deeply damage the oceans' ecosystems, and we can't even know the extent of the consequences. This is true because the oceans are so vast, making up 71 percent of the world's surface. Only a small portion of this space has been explored by humans, and our understanding of the deep is limited. Yet we do know that modern fishing methods inevitably reduce the biodiversity of the oceans, potentially wiping out species that have yet to be discovered. This is a dangerous situation for obvious reasons. As we have seen on land, humans are effectively stopping the course of evolution through extinction.

I believe there may have once been a time when humans lived in harmony with the environment, when our relationship with the natural world was one of give and take; however, with the development of an industrial society and the farming methods and consumer extravagance that have followed, our relationship with the earth has become bleak. These days most people look upon everything as a resource and find a way to exploit it for monetary profit. Eventually, if this continues, I believe civilization will collapse, and many will suffer. Instead of nurturing life, humans are destroying it, threatening all that we care deeply about, including our own existence. In our efforts to avoid this outcome, living sustainably is our privilege and responsibility.

> **Instead of nurturing life, humans are destroying it, threatening all that we care deeply about, including our own existence. In our efforts to avoid this outcome, living sustainably is our privilege and responsibility.**

THE BAD GUYS

RESEARCH

A Word on Vegan Nutrition

by Merryn Redenbach, physician and medical officer, *Steve Irwin*

The Sea Shepherd galley teams have a good understanding of vegan nutrition and health. They also know how to make food that looks so delicious, even people suffering from seasickness are tempted to try it.

Beyond satisfying both delicate and robust appetites, our experienced vegan cooks are savvy about important minerals and vitamins that can be insufficient in many modern diets. Nuts, seeds, green vegetables, chickpeas, and oranges are all good sources of calcium, for example. And nuts, seeds, oats, and legumes, including soy products, provide zinc, magnesium, and other minerals. (Gratefully, Sea Shepherd has received some great donations of raw and other vegan chocolate, which is high in magnesium.) Fortified soy milks are served in the galleys, providing enough vitamin B_{12} to get newbies through a campaign. However, because vegan diets are naturally low in vitamin B_{12}, I encourage vegans to take daily or weekly vitamin B_{12} supplements. Getting sufficient iron can be a challenge anywhere, particularly for women, although on some Sea Shepherd ships, the old iron water tanks surely provide some iron content.

It's important to eat foods containing vitamin C, such as citrus fruits, along with iron-rich foods to boost iron absorption. Vitamin C also is essential in preventing scurvy, so it's good that this vitamin is found in many fruits and vegetables. The galley teams are resourceful in making produce last. Even after months at sea, our meals feature fresh, vitamin-rich foods: there are always cabbages and carrots to sustain us. And in answer to a common question, no, we have not had a case of scurvy yet!

DESTINATION:
SOMEWHERE IN THE SOUTHERN OCEAN

There is much work to be done on the ships before we head to the Antarctic for our annual campaign to shut down the illegal Japanese whaling fleet. The final few weeks before we leave port are a manic frenzy of preparation.

The captain and first and second officers are responsible for overseeing the ship, dealing with the media, plotting the course, and checking that all the safety equipment is up-to-date. They also must run down their checklists and complete a mountain of paperwork so we can move in and out of port safely and efficiently.

The engineers race to make sure the engines are in tip-top condition. This includes filling up with fuel, topping up the tanks of lube oil, bringing all the appropriate parts and spares on board, and ensuring that the engines and generators are serviced and ready for a lot of use.

The deck crew and quartermasters work around the clock, tackling their seemingly endless list of responsibilities: maintaining security, servicing small-boat engines and deck equipment, chipping away rust and painting, organizing and testing safety equipment, tying down pretty much everything that could possibly move, training new crew, and assisting other crew members as needed. On top of all this, the deck crew handles the domestic chores, such as cleaning the heads (see page 22) and disposing of the trash.

Last but not least is the galley crew, and we're hustling too. Once we leave port there is no turning back, so we need to make sure the ship is fully stocked with enough food and beverages to satisfy fifty crew members for one hundred days. With the help of many hardworking crew members and onshore volunteers, we receive tens of thousands of dollars' worth of food supplies, most of which are donated by generous supporters. Next comes the daunting task of stowing everything away and firmly securing it so it won't move. We must assume that

We receive tens of thousands of dollars' worth of food supplies, most of which are donated by generous supporters.

we'll hit rough weather as soon as we leave port and that everything that can dislodge and go flying will do just that. So, for a start, we get busy tying down more than 1,500 pounds (700 kg) of flour, 1,300 pounds (600 kg) of potatoes, 1,100 pounds (500 kg) of onions, and 100 gallons (450 L) of nondairy milk, not to mention fifty cabbages and thirty pumpkins! In addition to securing these provisions, the galley crew is responsible for preparing and serving three hot meals plus snacks each day we're in port, as well as doing cleanup.

COOKING UP A STORM . . . IN A STORM

When I first began cooking at sea, we had limited means to predict the weather, and as a result we sailed into wild conditions at times. I've certainly had some memorable, rough rides and culinary adventures unique to life aboard ship. Even now, despite having detailed weather charts, we can't always avoid storms. In fact, whalers purposely lead us into bad weather to try and shake us off their tails. I'll tell you, on such days, it's *not* smooth sailing.

Sure, sure. You get the picture. But do you? How calmly would you cope if your kitchen suddenly defied the rules of gravity, heaving this way and that? How graceful would you be, struggling for a foothold and trying to contain the chaotic tumblings of stray pantry goods and cooking paraphernalia? Imagine this . . .

You: Taking the Galley by Storm

You wake up at 6:00 a.m. The weather is calm. So calm you hardly notice you're on a ship. You stroll into the galley and begin to prepare breakfast. Very gradually, over the next hour, the ship begins to roll. You adapt easily, as there's a rhythm to it. And you learn when it's safe to leave your station and then dart back in time to catch the oranges before they fall and roll away into the grotty unknown. So far, so good.

An hour later the swell picks up. The rolls are longer and deeper. You have to hold on to every item on the workbench. That's where the dishes you've managed to make thus far are tucked away.

Breakfast is served just as the gentle roll becomes a touch jerky. You nervously stand guard over the food, making sure nothing hits the deck, while people serve themselves. Phew. Breakfast is done!

Now you begin to prepare lunch. The weather picks up steadily, making this task go much slower than usual. The ship corkscrews up and down the waves. You become a little queazy. Your body feels heavy. Even walking from the sink to the workbench is a precarious adventure, and chopping an onion seems an impossible task. With all the energy you can muster, you get your jiggle on and blast out a one-pot wonder—a big pot of stew—with some salad and bread on the side. Another galley crew member spends two hours making cookies, which would normally take twenty minutes. Lunch is out by noon. Sigh. It's safe to breathe. For the moment.

Dinner's next. It's two hours into the prep and all you've managed to do is chop a few vegetables. And spill all the tahini dressing, remake it, and spill it again. So nix the tahini dressing, which isn't really practical on a day like today, you tell yourself. You gather your strength, crank the music—some kind of awful techno to get you moving—and charge on. You start cooking the beans, which are tightly secured and bubbling away on the stove. Then you spend twenty minutes struggling down the companionway to the dry storage area. You brace yourself, measuring out the rice and putting it into a huge pot. Slowly, you return to the galley, hoist the rice into the sink for washing, and then put it in the cooker for steaming.

The portholes (which are sealed tight) are under water every few seconds now, and you imagine that this is what it must be like to be inside a washing machine.

You're in the thick of the storm, and simply being in the galley is dangerous. The floor inevitably gets wet and becomes slippery. For quite a while, all you can do is hang on, taking care that you don't fall over, get stabbed by a knife, or get burned by a scalding pot or red-hot oven. Helpless, you can only laugh—how ridiculous it all is! The galley looks like a tornado has just torn through it.

Nonetheless, you and your galley mates have achieved the impossible: dinner. Very carefully, you transport it to the serving area. And just like that, the weather dies down and the sea becomes calm.

Folks cruise into the mess and look at the spread. Despite the colossal effort, it's not your finest work. The desserts alone tell the sad tale of your struggle: the cake has exploded out of the pan, and the pie, which took three hours to make, is lopsided. But the crew has already forgotten the storm as they curiously size up this weird excuse for a meal. Typical!

MORNING STARTERS

My work in the galley begins at 6:00 a.m. This is my favorite time of day. The ship is just about as quiet as an underway 1,017-ton diesel vessel can be! All I can hear is the chug of the engines and the smack of the waves slapping against the side of the ship. The first thing I do is turn on the ancient hot plates, which take a half hour to heat up. Around this time I like to go up on deck to catch the sunrise over the ocean, which is never disappointing. It's a time to prepare for what the day may bring.

The crew is usually slow moving and sleepy at breakfast, except for the folks who have just finished a four-hour shift in the engine room or on the bridge. The ship runs twenty-four hours a day, seven days a week, so there must always be a crew on duty in the engine room to make sure the engines are running smoothly and on the bridge to keep us on course and steer clear of icebergs. These duties are divided into four-hour watches, which means that breakfast is always somebody's lunch or dinner. For that reason, I make sure there's something hot in the mess every morning.

Southern Ocean Scramble

Tofu is a major treat when we're at sea, and we save it for special occasions, such as breakfast on New Year's Day. If you feel adventurous, experiment by adding different veggies and herbs.

2 pounds (900 g) firm silken tofu
⅓ cup (85 ml) olive oil
3 tablespoons (45 ml) thinly sliced fresh chives
4 teaspoons (20 ml) nutritional yeast flakes
2 cloves garlic, crushed
½ teaspoon (2 ml) ground turmeric
1 teaspoon (5 ml) salt
½ teaspoon (2 ml) freshly ground black pepper

MAKES 4 SERVINGS

Per serving:
299 calories
17 g protein
25 g fat (2 g sat)
6 g carbohydrates
611 mg sodium
62 mg calcium
3 g fiber

Drain the tofu and wrap it in an absorbent towel for 10 minutes to remove the excess moisture.

Put the tofu in a large bowl and mash it using a potato masher or wooden spoon. Add the oil, 1½ tablespoons (22 ml) of the chives, and the nutritional yeast, garlic, and turmeric and stir until well combined.

Cook in a large skillet over medium heat, turning the mixture occasionally with a metal spatula to prevent sticking, until lightly browned in spots, about 15 minutes.

Remove from the heat. Add the remaining 1½ tablespoons (22 ml) of chives and the salt and pepper and stir until evenly distributed. The tofu should resemble scrambled eggs.

SERVING SUGGESTION: Southern Ocean Scramble is perfect served on a thick slice of toasted sourdough bread.

Hot and Hearty Hash Browns

Here are some good ol' home-style hash brown potatoes. There's no better breakfast to warm you up and keep you going on a cold Antarctic morning.

2 tablespoons (30 ml) vegetable oil

5 medium russet potatoes, scrubbed (peeling optional) and cubed

½ red onion, sliced

¼ teaspoon (1 ml) freshly ground black pepper

¾ cup (185 ml) finely chopped fresh parsley (leaves only)

1 teaspoon (5 ml) salt

½ teaspoon (2 ml) dried thyme

Put the oil in a large skillet and heat over medium heat for 30 seconds. Add the potatoes, onion, and pepper and stir to combine. Cover and cook, turning the mixture with a metal spatula every 5 minutes, until the potatoes are lightly browned and fork-tender, about 15 minutes. Remove from the heat. Add the parsley, salt, and thyme and stir until evenly distributed.

MAKES 4 SERVINGS

Per serving:

210 calories

5 g protein

7 g fat (2 g sat)

31 g carbohydrates

589 mg sodium

0 mg calcium

5 g fiber

Shipshape Stewed Tomatoes

Stewed tomatoes provide a simple, healthy, and delicious start to the day, not to mention a great way to use up aging tomatoes. You can use less olive oil if you wish, but I recommend savoring this rich breakfast as is and following it with a light lunch.

8 tomatoes, quartered
¼ cup (60 ml) **olive oil**
2 tablespoons (30 ml) **coarsely chopped fresh basil**
2 cloves garlic, minced (or as much garlic as you can stand in the morning!)
Salt
Freshly ground black pepper

MAKES 4 SERVINGS

Per serving:
186 calories
3 g protein
14 g fat (1 g sat)
15 g carbohydrates
17 mg sodium
6 mg calcium
5 g fiber

Note: Analysis does not include salt and freshly ground black pepper to taste.

Put the tomatoes, oil, basil, and garlic in a large skillet. Cover and cook over medium-low heat, stirring occasionally, until the tomatoes are soft, 12 to 15 minutes. Remove from the heat and season with salt and pepper to taste.

SERVING SUGGESTION: Serve the tomatoes on thick slices of whole-grain toast.

Beans for Breakfast

Although canned baked beans are included in hearty breakfasts in many parts of the world, this fresh-cooked version is a much tastier alternative that can be served for breakfast, lunch, or dinner.

2 tablespoons (30 ml) olive oil

2 cloves garlic, thinly sliced

1 onion, finely diced

1 small red chile, minced

Pinch freshly ground black pepper

4 tomatoes, diced

2 tablespoons (30 ml) water

1½ tablespoons (22 ml) minced fresh parsley

1 tablespoon (15 ml) dried oregano

3 cups (750 ml) no-salt-added cooked or canned beans of your choice, rinsed and drained

1 teaspoon (5 ml) salt

Put the oil and garlic in a large, deep skillet over low heat and cook, stirring frequently, until the garlic begins to turn golden brown, about 2 minutes. Increase the heat to medium and add the onion, chile, and pepper. Cook, stirring frequently, for 5 minutes.

Stir in the tomatoes, water, 1 tablespoon (15 ml) of the parsley, and the oregano. Cook, stirring occasionally, for 10 minutes.

Add the beans, using a rubber spatula to fold them into the tomato mixture. Cook until the beans are fully heated through, 3 to 4 minutes. Remove from the heat and season with the salt. Garnish with the remaining ½ tablespoon (7 ml) of parsley.

SERVING SUGGESTION: Serve the beans on thick slices of whole-grain toast.

MAKES 4 SERVINGS

Per serving:

276 calories

12 g protein

8 g fat (1 g sat)

41 g carbohydrates

580 mg sodium

121 mg calcium

12 g fiber

Ship Speak

Landlubbers say:

Front of ship
Back of ship
Wheelhouse
Anchor chain locker
Top deck
Highest lookout
Bedroom
Floor
Ceiling
Wall
Corridor
Door
Window
Kitchen
Dining room
Living room
Wash-up area
Toilet
Left
Right

Sea Shepherds say:

Bow
Aft
Bridge
Ghost's hideout
Monkey deck
Crow's nest
Cabin
Deck
Deckhead
Bulkhead
Companionway
Hatch
Porthole
Galley
Mess
Saloon
Scullery
Head
Port
Starboard

On a ship, the "mess" is the dining room, so "eating in the mess" isn't as bad as it sounds. This is just one example of how new crew members must build up their vocabulary—often just to know where they are. It's almost like learning another language. Above are some of the other terms newbies have to get used to when they come aboard. (Oh—and eventually they also discover that the "ghost's hideout" is the anchor chain locker.)

Mainstay Blueberry Muffins

Muffins are wonderfully convenient snacks to have on hand, especially if you need to grab something substantial as you're running out the door—or into the wheelhouse for your morning shift. For a healthier option, use raw coconut sugar to replace the raw sugar and coconut oil to replace the vegetable oil.

2½ cups (625 ml) unbleached all-purpose flour

¾ cup (185 ml) raw sugar or raw coconut sugar

½ cup (125 ml) wheat germ

4 teaspoons (20 ml) baking powder

½ teaspoon (2 ml) salt

2¼ cups (560 ml) vegan buttermilk (see tip) or plain vegan yogurt

¾ cup (185 ml) vegetable oil or coconut oil

3 tablespoons (45 ml) applesauce

1 tablespoon (15 ml) molasses

1 cup (250 ml) fresh or frozen blueberries

MAKES 12 LARGE MUFFINS

Per muffin:

302 calories

5 g protein

15 g fat (5 g sat)

37 g carbohydrates

114 mg sodium

120 mg calcium

2 g fiber

Preheat the oven to 350 degrees F (180 degrees C). Line a standard 12-cup muffin tin with cupcake liners.

Sift the flour, sugar, wheat germ, baking powder, and salt into a large bowl. Stir with a dry whisk until well combined.

Put the buttermilk, oil, applesauce, and molasses in a small bowl. Stir until well combined.

Add the blueberries to the dry ingredients and stir until evenly distributed. Add the wet ingredients, using a rubber spatula to fold them into the dry ingredients until well combined.

Immediately spoon the batter into the lined muffin cups, filling each of them about three-quarters full. Bake for about 30 minutes, until a toothpick inserted in the center of a muffin comes out clean. Let cool in the pan before removing. Serve warm or at room temperature.

tip: To make vegan buttermilk, put 2¼ cups (560 ml) of plain unsweetened soy milk in a small bowl. Add 1 tablespoon (15 ml) of white vinegar and stir until well combined.

Creamy Coconut Oatmeal

Oats and cinnamon pair well to provide a bright and hearty beginning to any day. This recipe is soy-free and is served with coconut milk to create a smooth, rich creamy porridge.

3 cups (750 ml) water

2 cups (500 ml) old-fashioned rolled oats

1 (2-inch/5 cm) stick cinnamon

½ teaspoon (2 ml) vanilla extract

¼ teaspoon (1 ml) salt

1 banana, sliced (optional)

5 almonds, sliced (optional)

3 tablespoons (45 ml) full-fat coconut milk

MAKES 4 SERVINGS

Per serving:

158 calories

5 g protein

3 g fat (1 g sat)

27 g carbohydrates

148 mg sodium

20 mg calcium

4 g fiber

Note: Analysis does not include banana or almonds.

Put the water, oats, cinnamon stick, vanilla extract, and salt in a medium saucepan. Cook over medium heat, stirring occasionally, until the oatmeal is thick, about 8 minutes.

Spoon into four cereal bowls. Top each serving with the optional banana and almond slices and drizzle with the coconut milk.

Gilligan's Granola

My buddy Merri (or should I affectionately call her my "little buddy"?) gets the credit for creating all the following granola recipes, which she has whimsically named after everyone's favorite castaways. No doubt being shipwrecked is a lot more pleasant if you wash ashore with a fresh stash of your favorite breakfast fare.

10 cups (2.5 L) old-fashioned rolled oats

1½ cups (375 ml) unsalted raw or roasted peanuts

½ cup (125 ml) flaxseeds

½ cup (125 ml) raw sesame seeds

1 cup (250 ml) vegetable oil

½ cup (125 ml) unsalted natural peanut butter

½ cup (125 ml) granulated sugar

½ cup (125 ml) light brown sugar

¼ cup (60 ml) unsweetened cocoa powder

1 teaspoon (5 ml) ground cinnamon

½ teaspoon (2 ml) salt

1 cup (250 ml) unsweetened shredded dried coconut

½ cup (125 ml) vegan chocolate chips

½ cup (125 ml) unsweetened banana chips

Preheat the oven to 300 degrees F (150 degrees C).

Put the oats, peanuts, flaxseeds, and sesame seeds in a large bowl and stir until well combined.

Put the oil, peanut butter, granulated sugar, brown sugar, cocoa powder, cinnamon, and salt in a medium bowl and stir until well combined. Add to the oat mixture and stir until the oats are evenly coated.

Spread the mixture in a thin even layer on two large rimmed baking sheets. Bake for 10 minutes. Remove from the oven, stir, and bake for 10 minutes longer, or until the oats are toasted and lightly browned.

Let cool completely on the baking sheets. Divide the coconut, chocolate chips, and banana chips equally between both baking sheets and stir until evenly incorporated.

Transfer to storage containers and seal tightly. Stored in a cool, dark place, the granola will keep for 3 weeks.

MAKES 16 CUPS (4 L)

Per ½ cup:

264 calories

7 g protein

13 g fat (4 g sat)

31 g carbohydrates

7 mg sodium

45 mg calcium

5 g fiber

Mrs. Howell's Granola

Appropriately named after a millionaire's wife, this granola is rich. Pecans, dried cranberries, and aromatic spices add a bit of sophistication.

10 cups (2.5 L) old-fashioned rolled oats
1½ cups (375 ml) raw pecan pieces
1 cup (250 ml) raw sunflower seeds
½ cup (125 ml) flaxseeds
½ cup (125 ml) raw sesame seeds
1 cup (250 ml) vegetable oil
¾ cup (185 ml) granulated sugar
1 tablespoon (15 ml) ground cinnamon
1 teaspoon (5 ml) ground allspice
1 teaspoon (5 ml) ground cloves
½ teaspoon (2 ml) salt
1 cup (250 ml) unsweetened shredded dried coconut
1 cup (250 ml) dried cranberries
1 cup (250 ml) raisins

MAKES 18 CUPS (4.5 L)

Per ½ cup:
303 calories
5 g protein
16 g fat (5 g sat)
36 g carbohydrates
54 mg sodium
39 mg calcium
4 g fiber

Preheat the oven to 300 degrees F (150 degrees C).

Put the oats, pecans, sunflower seeds, flaxseeds, and sesame seeds in a large bowl and stir until well combined.

Put the oil, sugar, cinnamon, allspice, cloves, and salt in a medium bowl and stir until well combined. Add to the oat mixture and stir until the oats are evenly coated.

Spread the mixture in a thin even layer on two large rimmed baking sheets. Bake for 10 minutes. Remove from the oven, stir, and bake for 10 minutes longer, or until the oats are toasted and lightly browned.

Let cool completely on the baking sheets. Divide the coconut, cranberries, and raisins equally between both baking sheets and stir until evenly incorporated.

Transfer to storage containers and seal tightly. Stored in a cool, dark place, the granola will keep for 3 weeks.

Ginger's Granola

Like an auburn-haired starlet, this combo is captivating. Ground ginger and crystallized ginger both have starring roles, and they receive outstanding support from their nutty and fruity costars.

10 cups (2.5 L) old-fashioned rolled oats

1½ cups (375 ml) walnut pieces

1 cup (250 ml) raw sunflower seeds

½ cup (125 ml) flaxseeds

½ cup (125 ml) raw sesame seeds

1 cup (250 ml) vegetable oil

¾ cup (185 ml) granulated sugar

2 tablespoons (30 ml) ground ginger

½ teaspoon (2 ml) salt

2 cups (500 ml) dried cranberries

1 cup (250 ml) dried apricots, finely chopped

1 cup (250 ml) unsweetened shredded dried coconut

1 cup (250 ml) crystallized ginger, finely chopped

Preheat the oven to 300 degrees F (150 degrees C).

Put the oats, walnuts, sunflower seeds, flaxseeds, and sesame seeds in a large bowl and stir until well combined.

Put the oil, sugar, ground ginger, and salt in a medium bowl and stir until well combined. Add to the oat mixture and stir until the oats are evenly coated.

Spread the mixture in a thin even layer on two large rimmed baking sheets. Bake for 10 minutes. Remove from the oven, stir, and bake for 10 minutes longer, or until the oats are toasted and lightly browned.

Let cool completely on the baking sheets. Divide the cranberries, apricots, coconut, and crystallized ginger equally between both baking sheets and stir until evenly incorporated.

Transfer to storage containers and seal tightly. Stored in a cool, dark place, the granola will keep for 3 weeks.

MAKES 20 CUPS (5 L)

Per ½ cup:

287 calories

5 g protein

12 g fat (4 g sat)

40 g carbohydrates

52 mg sodium

45 mg calcium

4 g fiber

The Professor's Granola

Lightly sweetened with agave nectar, this classic granola is textbook. But don't let the simplicity of this formulation fool you. It earns an A+ every time.

8 cups (2 L) old-fashioned rolled oats
¼ cup (60 ml) walnut pieces
½ cup (125 ml) raw sunflower seeds
½ cup (125 ml) flaxseeds
½ cup (125 ml) raw sesame seeds
1 cup (250 ml) vegetable oil
½ cup (125 ml) light agave nectar
2 teaspoons (10 ml) ground cinnamon
½ teaspoon (2 ml) salt
1½ cups (375 ml) dried cranberries
1 cup (250 ml) unsweetened shredded dried coconut

MAKES 12 CUPS (3 L)

Per ½ cup:
412 calories
6 g protein
21 g fat (7 g sat)
52 g carbohydrates
66 mg sodium
47 mg calcium
6 g fiber

Preheat the oven to 300 degrees F (150 degrees C).

Put the oats, walnuts, sunflower seeds, flaxseeds, and sesame seeds in a large bowl and stir until well combined.

Put the oil, agave nectar, cinnamon, and salt in a medium bowl and stir until well combined. Add to the oat mixture and stir until the oats are evenly coated.

Spread the mixture in a thin even layer on two large rimmed baking sheets. Bake for 10 minutes. Remove from the oven, stir, and bake for 10 minutes longer, or until the oats are toasted and lightly browned.

Let cool completely on the baking sheets. Divide the cranberries and coconut equally between both baking sheets and stir until evenly incorporated.

Transfer to storage containers and seal tightly. Stored in a cool, dark place, the granola will keep for 3 weeks.

Mary Ann's Granola

Wholesome as the girl next door, this granola is subtly sweet, lightly spiced, and undeniably delightful. Free of fruits, this straightforward variation will never let you down.

10 cups (2.5 L) old-fashioned rolled oats

1½ cups (375 ml) raw almond slivers

1 cup (250 ml) raw sunflower seeds

½ cup (125 ml) flaxseeds

½ cup (125 ml) raw sesame seeds

1 cup (250 ml) vegetable oil

¾ cup (185 ml) granulated sugar

4 teaspoons (20 ml) ground cinnamon

1 teaspoon (5 ml) ground allspice

½ teaspoon (2 ml) salt

Preheat the oven to 300 degrees F (150 degrees C).

Put the oats, almonds, sunflower seeds, flaxseeds, and sesame seeds in a large bowl and stir until well combined.

Put the oil, sugar, cinnamon, allspice, and salt in a medium bowl and stir until well combined. Add to the oat mixture and stir until the oats are evenly coated.

Spread the mixture in a thin even layer on two large rimmed baking sheets. Bake for 10 minutes. Remove from the oven, stir, and bake for 10 minutes longer, or until the oats are toasted and lightly browned.

Let cool completely on the baking sheets. Transfer to storage containers and seal tightly. Stored in a cool, dark place, the granola will keep for 3 weeks.

MAKES 15 CUPS (3.75 L)

Per ½ cup:

242 calories

6 g protein

16 g fat (4 g sat)

22 g carbohydrates

53 mg sodium

61 mg calcium

5 g fiber

250F
République du Congo

Sound the Action Alarm!

This is the moment we've been waiting for. The call goes out to all crew, letting us know the whaling fleet is in sight. We prepare to engage.

A potential engagement with the whaling fleet usually unfolds like this: A ship will appear on our radar, or we may just have a good idea of where the target is, and the captain will deploy the helicopter to search the area. Because the visual range from the air is so much greater than it is from the ship, the helicopter pilot can often sight the whaling vessel, without being detected by the whalers. This puts us at a great advantage. Once the pilot has confirmed the ships are in fact the whale poachers, it's full steam ahead! The call goes out shipwide: "Target on radar. All hands prepare to engage!"

Each department carries out a different role. On the following page and sprinkled throughout the book are accounts by various crew members from each department, explaining their unique responses and duties during a campaign's first encounter with the whaling fleet.

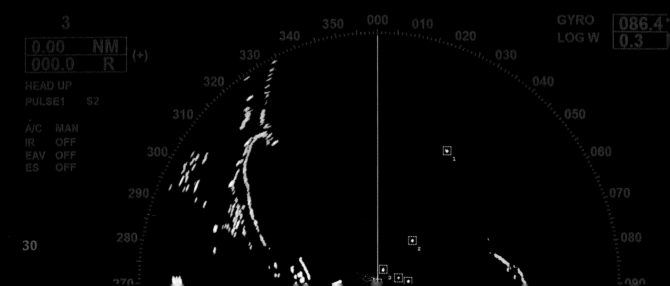

Pablo Watson, SECOND ENGINEER, *STEVE IRWIN*

After weeks of long summer days sailing past icebergs in the isolated Southern Ocean, I go down the steep steel stairs for another shift in the engine room. Midway through my shift, an unexpected call from the bridge drags me up from the depths below.

A frenzied voice blurts out at me: "There's a target on radar, something big. We think it's the *Nisshin*. We need two engines." I snap into action, going through the start-up procedures for our starboard engine and number-two generator so we can run our water cannon. Only after the machines are ready do I sit for a moment with my chief engineer. I allow the excitement to take over. "This is it," I hear myself say. He's smiling, and so am I.

The ship races at full speed, engines screaming their protest from below, and the bridge calls to say we're moving alongside the floating abattoir, the *Nisshin Maru*.

I stand by in our generator room, watching the temperature and pressures. Running everything this hard and hot has us all on edge; machines this old are prone to failures.

With oil cans and wrenches in hand, we wait nervously, feeling the ship roll from side to side as we maneuver about. It's David versus Goliath. It's David versus Goliath, and our slingshot is blazing in the Antarctic sunshine.

Chunky Beef, Barley, and Ale Stew,
page 62

SOUPS

What I decide to cook from day to day depends on a number of factors. I always try to use up fresh foods that are just about to turn bad. And I always respect the weather. Although making soup is a great way to clear out aging produce, doing so is not an option during a stormy gale. When I see waves slamming against the porthole, I strike soup from the menu. However, when the weather calms down, a nice big bowl of piping hot soup is the perfect way to warm up a fellow crew member who has spent a long day zigzagging around the ice, harassing whale poachers.

Captain's Habitat Split Pea Soup

I asked Captain Paul if he'd share a few of his favorite recipes. This one was a staple dish for him when he was growing up in Saint Andrews, New Brunswick, Canada. It's easy to prepare and brimming with rich and subtle flavors.

8 cups (2 L) water
2 cups (500 ml) dried yellow split peas, rinsed and drained
1½ cups (375 ml) diced celery
1 cup (250 ml) chopped onion
¼ cup (60 ml) chopped fresh curly parsley (stems and leaves)
2 cloves garlic, crushed
½ teaspoon (2 ml) salt
½ teaspoon (2 ml) freshly ground black pepper

MAKES 4 SERVINGS

Per serving:
247 calories
21 g protein
0 g fat (0 g sat)
61 g carbohydrates
359 mg sodium
80 mg calcium
25 g fiber

Put all the ingredients in a large soup pot and stir to combine. Bring to a boil over medium-high heat. Decrease the heat to medium-low, partially cover, and cook, stirring occasionally, until the peas are tender, 30 to 40 minutes.

If you prefer a thinner soup, add more water until the desired thickness is achieved. For a creamier soup, remove from the heat and partially blend with an immersion blender (see below).

SERVING SUGGESTION: Serve with a drizzle of olive oil and a pinch of additional black pepper.

How to Blend Scalding Soup

Aboard ship, blending hot soup can be a very dangerous activity. One ocean wave can cause a sudden spill in the galley—and a potentially severe burn for the cook.

I minimize the handling of steaming soups by using an immersion blender when I want the soup to be creamy and smooth. Whether at sea or in your own kitchen, you can use this convenient tool by submerging it right in the soup pot after the ingredients are cooked. Just remove the pot from the heat before blending.

Alternatively, blend the soup using a standing blender. Transfer the cooked ingredients in small batches to the blender, filling the container no more than half full. Begin processing on a low setting and gently pulse until the desired consistency is achieved. Be sure to leave the container lid slightly ajar to allow steam to escape. As it's processed, steaming soup can force the lid right off the container, creating a burn hazard.

Red Lentil, Lemon, and Rosemary Soup

This recipe was inspired by our ship's doctor, Merryn. Delicious and nutritious, this soup proves that our doctor has a lot more to offer the galley crew than bandages and burn creams.

3 cups (750 ml) dried red lentils, picked over, rinsed, and drained
9 cups (2.25 L) water
1½ tablespoons (22 ml) fresh rosemary leaves, or 1½ teaspoons (7 ml) dried
¼ cup (60 ml) olive oil
Zest of 1 lemon
Juice of 1 lemon
Salt
Freshly ground black pepper

Put the lentils in a large soup pot and cover with the water. Bring to a boil over medium-high heat. Decrease the heat to medium-low and stir in the rosemary. Partially cover and cook, stirring occasionally, until the lentils are very soft, 25 to 30 minutes. Remove from the heat. Stir in the oil, zest, and juice. Season with salt and pepper to taste.

MAKES 4 SERVINGS

Per serving:
663 calories
39 g protein
14 g fat (1 g sat)
94 g carbohydrates
0.7 mg sodium
63 mg calcium
27 g fiber

Note: Analysis does not include salt and freshly ground black pepper to taste.

Spicy Greek Lentil Soup

Lightly cooked greens and red lentils find wedded bliss in this quick and easy classic. You can go lighter or heavier on the chiles, depending on your heat tolerance.

2 tablespoons (30 ml) olive oil

4 cloves garlic, thinly sliced

1 can (14 ounces/397 ml) no-salt-added whole peeled tomatoes

3 Thai chiles with seeds, minced

6 cups (1.5 L) water

2 cups (500 ml) dried red lentils, picked over, rinsed, and drained

½ teaspoon (2 ml) salt

½ teaspoon (2 ml) freshly ground black pepper

2 cups (500 ml) chopped baby greens (spinach, chard, or kale), lightly packed

MAKES 4 SERVINGS

Per serving:
437 calories
29 g protein
8 g fat (1 g sat)
66 g carbohydrates
289 mg sodium
8 mg calcium
19 g fiber

Note: Analysis does not include salt and freshly ground black pepper to taste.

Put the oil and garlic in a large soup pot over medium heat and cook, stirring frequently, until the garlic begins to brown, about 2 minutes. Add the tomatoes and chiles and cook, stirring occasionally, for 5 minutes. Add the water, lentils, salt, and pepper. Partially cover and cook, stirring occasionally, until the lentils are tender, 25 to 30 minutes. Remove from the heat and stir in the greens. Serve immediately to ensure the greens remain bright green.

Blue Whale
Balaenoptera musculus
WWF

50c
Australia

Tuscan White Bean Soup

Resplendent with fresh and aromatic herbs, this soup has the power to transport cold and weary campaigners (or at least their taste buds) to the warm and sunny Italian countryside.

2 tablespoons (30 ml) olive oil

5 cloves garlic, thinly sliced

½ red onion, sliced

1 tablespoon (15 ml) chopped fresh sage, or 1 teaspoon (5 ml) rubbed sage

1 tablespoon (15 ml) chopped fresh rosemary, or 1 teaspoon (5 ml) dried

5 cups (1.25 L) no-salt-added vegetable broth

15 cherry tomatoes, quartered

3 cups (750 ml) no-salt-added cooked or canned white beans, rinsed and drained

20 French green beans, chopped into 2-inch (5 cm) lengths

1 tablespoon (15 ml) chopped fresh flat-leaf parsley

Salt

Freshly ground black pepper

Put the oil and garlic in a large soup pot over medium heat and cook, stirring frequently, until the garlic begins to brown, about 2 minutes. Add the onion, sage, and rosemary and cook, stirring occasionally, until the onion begins to soften, about 5 minutes. Add the broth and tomatoes and stir to combine. Cover, bring to a boil, and decrease the heat to medium-low. Add the white beans, green beans, and parsley and cook, stirring occasionally, until the green beans are tender, about 8 minutes. Remove from the heat and season with salt and pepper to taste.

SERVING SUGGESTION: Pair each serving of steaming soup with a thick slice of crusty bread.

MAKES 4 SERVINGS

Per serving:

256 calories

13 g protein

9 g fat (1 g sat)

41 g carbohydrates

166 mg sodium

116 mg calcium

16 g fiber

Tips for Seasick Seafolk

Well over half the crew experiences seasickness during the first few days at sea, and some unfortunates never get their sea legs, but this is rare. Among those who succumb, symptoms vary from feeling extremely tired and lethargic to not being able to get out of bed at all. The only way I can think of to describe seasickness is to say that it's like being really hungover but still dizzy drunk at the same time—so basically the worst feeling imaginable!

Nausea is one of the hallmarks of seasickness. It seems as though every seafarer has a different and strange remedy for nausea, but most agree that ginger is a great comfort for the tummy. This classic cure is one you can drink down: grate a little piece of fresh ginger, stir it into a glass of warm fizzy water, and bottoms up. Then there are those who take it straight: Brian, one of our engineers, likes to carry a piece of ginger around in his front pocket and nibble on it throughout the day.

Our medical officer, Merryn, prefers the prescription drug Phenergan, which works well for motion sickness and nausea. My recommendation is to get out on deck if the weather permits and feel the fresh air and salty spray on your skin. Looking at the horizon helps too. I think of seasickness this way: It makes sense that our bodies are yelling at us, freaking out, and wondering what's going on. Naturally, a body needs time to adjust to a new environment and recover from its confusion.

People who never suffer from seasickness can be unsympathetic. For example, captain Paul Watson barely acknowledges its existence. He likes to quote comic Spike Milligan, who wrote: "A sure cure for seasickness is to sit under a tree."

Warming Pumpkin Soup

Fresh pumpkins keep for a long time, so we tend to eat a lot of this soup toward the end of a campaign. Pumpkin is such a fabulous vegetable, remaining colorful and nutritious even after three months at sea!

¼ cup (60 ml) vegetable oil

1 onion, diced

1 cup (250 ml) diced celery

2 cloves garlic, whole

½ teaspoon (2 ml) freshly ground black pepper

1 bay leaf

4 cups (1 L) no-salt-added vegetable broth

2½ cups (625 ml) peeled and cubed pumpkin

2 cups (500 ml) peeled and cubed potatoes

1½ cups (375 ml) peeled and cubed carrots

1 cup (250 ml) full-fat coconut milk

1 teaspoon (5 ml) ground cumin

¼ teaspoon (1 ml) ground cinnamon

Salt

Freshly ground black pepper

Heat the oil in a large soup pot over medium heat. Add the onion, celery, garlic, pepper, and bay leaf and cook, stirring frequently, until the onion is soft and translucent, about 10 minutes. Add the broth, pumpkin, potatoes, and carrots and stir to combine. Bring to a boil over medium-high heat. Decrease the heat to medium-low, cover, and cook, stirring occasionally, until the vegetables are soft, about 20 minutes.

Remove from the heat. Add the coconut milk, cumin, and cinnamon and stir until well incorporated. Blend the soup until creamy and smooth using an immersion blender or standing blender (see sidebar, page 34). Season with salt and pepper to taste. Remove the bay leaf before serving.

SERVING SUGGESTION: For a special touch when serving, drizzle toasted pumpkin seed oil over the soup or garnish it with toasted pumpkin seeds.

MAKES 4 SERVINGS

Per serving:

378 calories

4 g protein

25 g fat (4 g sat)

37 g carbohydrates

114 mg sodium

52 mg calcium

7 g fiber

Note: Analysis does not include salt and freshly ground black pepper to taste.

Chickpea Noodle Soup for the Vegan Soul

The ultimate cold-weather comfort food, this soup is guaranteed to leave you feeling satisfied. It packs a particular punch thanks to the addition of nori, a sea vegetable that is not only flavorful but also a rich source of protein, iron, and vitamin C.

8 cups (2 L) no-salt added vegetable or vegan chicken-style broth

1 tablespoon (15 ml) vegan butter

2 cups (500 ml) finely diced leeks (tender green parts only)

2 cups (500 ml) finely chopped celery (including leaves)

3 cloves garlic, minced

1/2 teaspoon (2 ml) crushed red chile flakes

1/2 teaspoon (2 ml) dried thyme

1 cup (250 ml) no-salt-added cooked or canned chickpeas, rinsed, drained, and lightly mashed or chopped

1 cup (250 ml) fresh or frozen corn kernels

1 sheet nori, cut into thin, short strips

2 tablespoons (30 ml) nutritional yeast flakes

4 ounces (113 g) rice noodles

Salt

Freshly ground black pepper

Minced fresh parsley, for garnish

MAKES 4 SERVINGS

Per serving:
193 calories
6 g protein
4 g fat (1 g sat)
35 g carbohydrates
128 mg sodium
35 mg calcium
4 g fiber

Note: Analysis does not include salt and freshly ground black pepper to taste or parsley for garnish.

Put the broth in a large soup pot and bring to a simmer over medium-high heat.

While the broth is warming, put the butter in a large skillet over medium-high heat. When the butter is melted, add the leeks, celery, and garlic and cook, stirring frequently, until the leeks are soft, about 10 minutes. Add the chile flakes and thyme and cook, stirring frequently, for 5 minutes.

Add the leek mixture to the broth and stir to combine. Add the chickpeas, corn, nori, and nutritional yeast and cook, stirring occasionally, for 20 minutes.

Prepare the rice noodles according to the package instructions. Drain the noodles in a colander and rinse with cold water. Add the noodles to the soup and cook, stirring occasionally, for 1 to 2 minutes. Season with salt and pepper to taste. Serve immediately, garnished with parsley.

Cream of Mushroom Soup

If you're looking to impress folks who are having a hard time ditching dairy products, this recipe has the power to convert. Because this savory soup is quite rich, I recommend serving it in small portions as an appetizer.

¼ cup (60 ml) olive oil
½ onion, finely diced
3 cloves garlic, minced
6 cups (1.5 L) finely diced button mushrooms (about 30)
2½ teaspoons (12 ml) fresh thyme, or 1 teaspoon (2 ml) dried
3 cups (750 ml) water
1 cup (250 ml) dry white wine
Salt
½ cup (125 ml) vegan cream cheese
Freshly ground black pepper

MAKES 5 SERVINGS

Per serving:
219 calories
5 g protein
15 g fat (1 g sat)
7 g carbohydrates
104 mg sodium
10 mg calcium
1 g fiber

Note: Analysis does not include salt and freshly ground black pepper to taste.

Put the oil, onion, and garlic in a large soup pot over medium heat and cook, stirring frequently, until the onion begins to soften, about 5 minutes. Add the mushrooms and thyme and cook, stirring occasionally, until the mushrooms are soft, about 15 minutes. Add the water, wine, and a pinch of salt and cook, stirring occasionally, for 10 minutes.

Remove from the heat. Stir in the cream cheese and season with salt and pepper to taste. If desired, reheat over medium-low heat, stirring occasionally, until hot. For a smoother soup, partially blend with an immersion blender (see sidebar, page 34).

DELPHINAPTERUS LEUCAS

Roasted Red Pepper and Tomato Soup

Roasting is a great way to bring out the deep flavors of fresh vegetables. This soup is beautiful, colorful, and delectable: a wonderful and warming way to deliver nutrients to a hungry, hardworking body.

8 tomatoes, quartered

3 large red bell peppers, each cut into 8 pieces

3 large yellow bell peppers, each cut into 8 pieces

1 onion, sliced

8 cloves garlic

2 Thai chiles with seeds, halved

2 teaspoons (10 ml) paprika

1/2 teaspoon (2 ml) salt

1/2 teaspoon (2 ml) freshly ground black pepper

1/3 cup (85 ml) olive oil

3 cups (750 ml) no-salt-added vegetable broth

3 cups (750 ml) plain unsweetened nondairy milk

3 tablespoons (45 ml) no-salt-added tomato paste

Preheat the oven to 400 degrees F (205 degrees C).

Put the tomatoes, red bell peppers, yellow bell peppers, onion, garlic, and chiles in a deep baking dish. Sprinkle with the paprika, salt, and pepper. Drizzle with the oil and stir until the vegetables are evenly coated with the oil and spices. Bake for 20 minutes, or until the vegetables are tender and beginning to turn black around the edges.

Transfer the roasted vegetables, including the oil, to a large soup pot. Add the broth, milk, and tomato paste and stir to combine. Bring to a boil over medium-high heat, stirring occasionally. Remove from the heat.

Blend the soup until creamy using an immersion blender or standing blender (see sidebar, page 34). If desired, reheat over medium-low heat, stirring occasionally, until hot.

MAKES 4 SERVINGS

Per serving:

341 calories

7 g protein

20 g fat (2 g sat)

42 g carbohydrates

469 mg sodium

37 mg calcium

6 g fiber

Polar Potato and Leek Soup

Potatoes go the distance—all the way to the Antarctic! Since they keep in storage for a long time, they're a dietary staple during long ship voyages. Creamy and warming, this soup will keep you full for hours.

5 cups (1.25 L) chopped leeks (tender green parts only)

1 tablespoon (15 ml) vegan butter

1 tablespoon (15 ml) vegetable oil

2 cloves garlic, chopped

1 teaspoon (5 ml) onion powder

1 teaspoon (5 ml) reduced-sodium tamari

1/2 teaspoon (2 ml) freshly ground black pepper

3 medium potatoes, peeled and diced

3 cups (750 ml) water

1/2 teaspoon (2 ml) salt

1 cup (250 ml) full-fat coconut milk

1/4 cup (60 ml) thinly sliced fresh chives, plus more for garnish

MAKES 4 SERVINGS

Per serving:
326 calories
6 g protein
17 g fat (1 g sat)
38 g carbohydrates
420 mg sodium
9 mg calcium
4 g fiber

Put the leeks, butter, oil, garlic, onion powder, tamari, and pepper in a large soup pot and cook over medium heat, stirring frequently, until the leeks are soft, about 10 minutes.

Add the potatoes, water, and salt and stir to combine. Bring to a boil over medium-high heat. Decrease the heat to medium-low and cook, stirring occasionally, until the potatoes are soft, about 20 minutes. Remove from the heat. Stir in the coconut milk and chives.

Blend the soup until thick and creamy using an immersion blender or standing blender (see sidebar, page 34). If desired, reheat over medium-low heat, stirring occasionally, until hot. Garnish each bowl with a pinch of chives.

Clear Skies Cleansing Soup

This is the ticket when you and your crew are on a health kick. Simple, clean, and satisfying.

- 10 cups (2.5 L) no-salt-added vegetable broth
- 6 cups (1.5 L) cauliflower florets
- 2 sweet potatoes, peeled and diced
- 1 clove garlic, minced
- 6 cups (1.5 L) broccoli, separated into florets
- Zest of 2 lemons
- Juice of 2 lemons
- 1 tablespoon (15 ml) thinly sliced fresh chives
- 6 cups (1.5 L) stemmed baby spinach, lightly packed
- Salt
- Freshly ground black pepper

Put the broth, cauliflower, sweet potatoes, and garlic in a large soup pot over medium heat. Cover and cook until the vegetables are tender, about 20 minutes. Decrease the heat to medium-low and add the broccoli, zest, juice, and chives. Partially cover and cook until the broccoli is tender, about 10 minutes. Remove from the heat and stir in the spinach.

Blend the soup until creamy using an immersion blender or standing blender (see sidebar, page 34). Season with salt and pepper to taste. If desired, reheat over medium-low heat, stirring occasionally, until hot.

MAKES 4 SERVINGS

Per serving:

240 calories

17 g protein

0 g fat (0 g sat)

50 g carbohydrates

208 mg sodium

29 mg calcium

17 g fiber

Note: Analysis does not include salt and freshly ground black pepper to taste.

SEA SHEPHERD

MAINS

Lunch and dinner are fairly large meals for us. When the weather begins to get cold, the crew members who work outside show a notable increase in appetite. To keep them going between lunch and dinner, the galley crew also serves afternoon tea, which is usually some kind of sweet.

Sea Shepherd's Pie

We couldn't have an official Sea Shepherd cookbook without including our signature dish, Sea Shepherd's Pie. Perfect for entertaining, this one-dish wonder can easily be made in advance and baked later in the day. Consider it your go-to entrée when you don't want to be stuck in the kitchen—or galley—if you can be enjoying good company instead.

FILLING

1 tablespoon (15 ml) vegetable oil

1 tablespoon (15 ml) vegan butter

3 cups (750 ml) sliced button mushrooms

1 leek, thinly sliced (tender green parts only)

1 onion, diced

1 carrot, peeled and diced

1 stalk celery, finely diced

3 cloves garlic, minced

3 tablespoons (45 ml) reduced-sodium tamari

1 teaspoon (5 ml) freshly ground black pepper

3 cups (750 ml) no-salt-added vegetable broth or water, plus more as needed

3 cups (750 ml) dried French lentils, picked over, rinsed, and drained

2 tomatoes, finely diced

1 tablespoon (15 ml) cider vinegar

1 tablespoon (15 ml) nutritional yeast flakes

TOPPING

4 potatoes, peeled and diced

1 tablespoon (15 ml) olive oil, plus more for drizzling

Pinch salt

1 tablespoon (15 ml) thinly sliced fresh chives

MAKES 6 SERVINGS

Per serving:
537 calories
26 g protein
6 g fat (1 g sat)
67 g carbohydrates
726 mg sodium
70 mg calcium
14 g fiber

To make the filling, put the oil and butter in a large soup pot over medium-high heat until the butter is melted. Decrease the heat to medium and add the mushrooms, leek, onion, carrot, celery, and garlic and cook, stirring frequently, until soft, about 10 minutes. Add the tamari and pepper and cook, stirring occasionally, for 8 minutes.

Add the broth, lentils, and tomatoes and bring to a boil over medium-high heat. Decrease the heat to medium, partially cover, and cook, stirring occasionally, until the lentils are tender, about 25 minutes. If necessary, add more broth as the lentils cook so they don't become dry. Stir in the vinegar and nutritional yeast. Transfer to a 4-quart (4 L) casserole.

Preheat the oven to 400 degrees F (205 degrees C).

While the lentils cook, prepare the topping. Fill a medium saucepan with water and bring to a boil over high heat. Add the potatoes, partially cover, and cook until soft, about 15 minutes. Drain. Add the oil and salt and mash until the potatoes are smooth and creamy.

Spread the topping evenly over the filling. Sprinkle the chives evenly over the topping and drizzle with olive oil. Bake for 20 minutes, until golden brown and bubbly.

SERVING SUGGESTION: Serve hot, covered in Punk Rock Gravy (page 106) and with a side of steamed vegetables.

Dr. Merryn Redenbach, MEDICAL OFFICER, *STEVE IRWIN*

The crew rejoices in its first glimpse of the whaling fleet, because it means we're getting close to our goal of protecting the whales from the poachers. But it also increases the chances of confrontation—either for our small boats or larger vessels.

For the medical team, this sighting is a reality check: are we prepared for the possible dangers? Like preparing food at sea, providing medical care has particular challenges. There are many potential scenarios: What if someone falls from a small boat and experiences hypothermia? What if crew members are exposed to tear gas or hit by projectiles? Someone could be seriously injured on a lower or upper deck, in the engine room, or down in a hold. And if a crew member is injured far away from the main ship, out on a small boat, how do we assess whether the action should stop so we can get them back safely for medical care?

In response to any number of emergent situations, we have to quickly recognize exactly what supplies we need and how to respond. We need to have emergency supplies organized and accessible in grab-and-go bags.

Because we're at sea for months at a time with no access to outside medical care, it's important we have all we need to set up a mini-hospital. We're stocked with everything from antibiotics to bandages, pain meds to stretchers. We even have a defibrillator, a device that shocks the heart back into action. Luckily, we have never had any serious injuries on board. Still, at all times, we need to be prepared, be flexible, and think on

Oceangoing Onion Pie

Dan is a robotics engineer and the ship's second engineer. Following is my version of his mother's onion pie. Because I strayed a bit from the original recipe, Dan calls this my "murder" of onion pie. But none of the other crew complain.

3 tablespoons (45 ml) vegan butter

5 onions, diced

½ cup (125 ml) plain unsweetened nondairy milk

3 tablespoons (45 ml) couscous

1 teaspoon (5 ml) ground nutmeg

1 cup (250 ml) stemmed baby spinach, packed

Salt

Freshly ground black pepper

14 sheets (about 4 ounces/113 g) phyllo dough (see tip)

MAKES 6 SERVINGS

Per serving:

177 calories

4 g protein

7 g fat (1 g sat)

25 g carbohydrates

161 mg sodium

8 mg calcium

3 g fiber

Note: Analysis does not include salt and freshly ground black pepper to taste.

Put the butter in a large soup pot over medium heat. When the butter is melted, add the onions and cook, stirring frequently, until soft and translucent, about 10 minutes. Add the milk, couscous, and nutmeg and cook, stirring occasionally, until the couscous is soft and has absorbed most of the liquid, 10 to 15 minutes. Remove from the heat, stir in the spinach, and season with salt and pepper to taste.

Preheat the oven to 350 degree F (180 degrees C).

Line the bottom and sides of a 10-inch (25 cm) pie plate with 8 sheets of the phyllo dough. The dough will hang over the pie plate. Spoon the onion mixture into the lined pie plate. Lay the remaining phyllo dough on top and fold the overhanging dough up on top of the pie. Bake for 45 minutes, or until the phyllo dough is golden brown.

tip: Immediately cover the phyllo dough with plastic wrap, then a damp towel, when you unroll thawed dough. Keep covered until needed. Do not leave the phyllo dough uncovered for more than 1 minute to prevent it from drying out.

Creamy Oceangoing Onion Pie: Add ½ pound (225 g) of mashed silken tofu with the milk, couscous, and nutmeg.

Dolphins on the Bow!

When someone spots dolphins riding our wake, the news very quickly spreads throughout the ship. We all bolt to the bow and lean over the railing to take a look. These welcome interactions are not just fantastic to see—they're also loud! We greet the cheeky clicks and squeaks of our aquatic friends with yelps and whoops of pure delight.

Revolutionary Vegetable Crumble

So many childhood favorites are a cinch to veganize. Here's one of mine. It's a wholesome and complete meal that can be made nut-free by simply replacing the mixed nuts with mixed seeds.

CRUMBLE TOPPING

1½ cups (375 ml) whole wheat flour

¼ cup (60 ml) vegan butter

1 cup (250 ml) grated vegan cheddar-style cheese

½ cup (125 ml) mixed raw nuts, ground or finely chopped

2 tablespoons (30 ml) raw sesame seeds

FILLING

2 tablespoons (30 ml) vegan butter

1 onion, diced

5 cups (1.25 L) peeled and cubed mixed root vegetables

1¼ cups (310 ml) no-salt-added vegetable broth

¼ cup (60 ml) unbleached all-purpose flour

¾ cup (185 ml) plain unsweetened nondairy milk

3 tablespoons (45 ml) minced fresh parsley

Salt

Freshly ground black pepper

MAKES 6 SERVINGS

Per serving:

440 calories

12 g protein

22 g fat (5 g sat)

53 g carbohydrates

349 mg sodium

106 mg calcium

11 g fiber

Note: Analysis does not include salt and freshly ground black pepper to taste.

To make the crumble topping, put the flour and butter in a large bowl. Cut the butter into the flour using a pastry knife or fork until the mixture resembles coarse crumbs. Add the cheese, nuts, and sesame seeds and stir until well combined. Set aside.

To make the filling, put the butter in a large saucepan over medium heat. When the butter is melted, add the onion and cook, stirring frequently, until soft and translucent, about 10 minutes. Add the vegetables, cover, and cook, stirring occasionally, until the vegetables just start to soften, about 10 minutes.

Preheat the oven to 350 degrees F (180 degrees C).

Put the broth and flour in a small bowl and stir until the flour is dissolved. Add the flour mixture, milk, and parsley to the vegetables and stir to combine. Cook, stirring occasionally, until the vegetables are tender, about 15 minutes. Season with salt and pepper to taste.

Transfer the filling to a 4-quart (4 L) casserole dish. Sprinkle the crumble topping evenly over the top. Bake for 30 minutes, or until golden brown.

First Mate Mushroom and Kale Sauté

Dried mushrooms are welcome staples aboard ship. They're hearty, flavorful, and pair well with many ingredients, such as greens.

3 ounces (85 g) dried sliced shiitake mushrooms

1 teaspoon (5 ml) vegetable oil

2 tablespoons (30 ml) reduced-sodium tamari

5 cups (1.25 L) stemmed and coarsely chopped kale, lightly packed

¼ head Chinese cabbage, shredded

½ cup (125 ml) sliced green onions

2 teaspoons (10 ml) raw sesame seeds

Put the mushrooms in a large bowl and cover with boiling water. Cover and let soak until fully hydrated, about 10 minutes. Drain and use your hands to squeeze out any excess liquid.

Put the oil, tamari, and mushrooms in a large skillet over high heat and cook, stirring almost constantly, until the mushrooms are soft, about 8 minutes. Add the kale, cabbage, green onions, and sesame seeds and cook until the greens are tender, 5 to 10 minutes.

SERVING SUGGESTION: Serve over hot steamed rice with Old Salt (and Pepper) Tofu (page 59).

MAKES 4 SERVINGS

Per serving:

196 calories

13 g protein

4 g fat (1 g sat)

24 g carbohydrates

425 mg sodium

88 mg calcium

5 g fiber

Savory Pancakes with Satay Sauce

Oh, the elegance! These pancakes, with their savory sauce, add sophistication to any dinner table. On a practical note, we seafarers favor these pancakes for their high vitamin-C content, which helps to ward off scurvy.

SATAY SAUCE

¾ cup (185 ml) unsalted natural crunchy peanut butter

¼ cup (60 ml) hot water, plus more as needed

4 teaspoons (20 ml) reduced-sodium tamari

2 teaspoons (10 ml) toasted sesame oil

1 clove garlic, crushed

1 teaspoon (5 ml) seeded and minced hot green chile

1 teaspoon (5 ml) curry powder

PANCAKES

6 cups (1.5 L) thinly sliced cabbage

1 onion, thinly sliced

1 carrot, peeled and grated

2 cups (500 ml) unbleached all-purpose flour

1 tablespoon (15 ml) baking powder

1 teaspoon (5 ml) salt

1½ cups (375 ml) plain unsweetened nondairy milk

1 cup (250 ml) water

2 tablespoons (30 ml) vegetable oil, plus more for the skillet

MAKES 4 SERVINGS

Per serving:
691 calories
23 g protein
35 g fat (6 g sat)
69 g carbohydrates
1,090 mg sodium
295 mg calcium
9 g fiber

To make the sauce, put all the ingredients in a small bowl and stir until well combined. If a thinner sauce is desired, add more hot water, 1 tablespoon (15 ml) at a time, until the desired consistency is achieved. Set aside.

To make the pancakes, put the cabbage, onion, and carrot in a large bowl.

Sift the flour, baking powder, and salt into a separate large bowl. Whisk in the milk, water, and oil until the mixture is smooth. Add the vegetables to the flour mixture and stir until well combined.

Lightly coat a skillet (cast iron if you have one) with oil and heat over medium-high heat. Spoon ¼ cup (60 ml) of batter per pancake into the skillet and cook until the bottom of the pancakes are golden brown, about 5 minutes. (You will need to cook the pancakes in a few batches, depending on the size of the skillet.) Flip the pancakes over and cook the other side until golden

brown, about 5 minutes. Repeat with the remaining batter, adjusting the heat as necessary.

Divide the Satay Sauce among four small bowls and serve alongside the pancakes for dipping.

tip: To keep the pancakes warm while the remainder cook, preheat the oven to 200 degrees F (93 degrees C). Line a baking sheet with parchment paper. When the oven is preheated, put the baking sheet in the oven and begin cooking the pancakes on the stove top. Transfer each cooked pancake to the baking sheet using a metal spatula.

SERVING SUGGESTION: Many delectable items can accent this dish. Possible garnishes include chopped fresh cilantro leaves, nori flakes, pickled ginger, and sweet soy sauce.

Even-Keel Kabobs with Dipping Sauce

Kabobs are always a colorful and welcome addition in our ship's mess, and they'll get raves at your barbecue or potluck too. Experiment with different kinds of vegetables or try using tempeh instead of tofu. To promote even cooking, make the sizes and shapes of the various ingredients as consistent as possible.

KABOBS

12 cherry tomatoes, whole

12 button mushrooms, whole

1 pound (450 g) super-firm or extra-firm tofu, cut into 12 cubes

12 cubes pineapple

12 cubes zucchini

12 pieces red onion

12 pieces red bell pepper

12 pieces green bell pepper

MARINADE

½ cup (125 ml) no-salt-added vegan chicken-style broth

3 tablespoons (45 ml) olive oil

1½ tablespoons (22 ml) minced fresh parsley

1 tablespoon (15 ml) sesame seeds, lightly toasted

1 clove garlic, minced

Pinch salt

Pinch freshly ground black pepper

DIPPING SAUCE

¼ cup (60 ml) plain unsweetened nondairy milk

¼ cup (60 ml) tahini

¼ cup (60 ml) finely chopped cilantro

2 tablespoons (30 ml) olive oil

Zest of ½ lemon

Juice of ½ lemon

1 teaspoon (5 ml) nutritional yeast flakes (optional)

½ clove garlic, minced

MAKES 12 LARGE SKEWERS, 6 SERVINGS

Per serving:
285 calories
13 g protein
19 g fat (3 g sat)
17 g carbohydrates
27 mg sodium
134 mg calcium
5 g fiber

To make the kabobs, put one of each ingredient on each of twelve skewers, switching up the order of ingredients from skewer to skewer. Put the kabobs on a rimmed baking sheet.

To make the marinade, put the broth, oil, parsley, sesame seeds, and garlic in a small bowl and stir until well combined. Pour over the kabobs, sprinkle with the salt and pepper, cover with plastic wrap, and let marinate for 2 hours, turning every 30 minutes.

Preheat a grill (if using the stove top, see tip). Cook the kabobs, brushing occasionally with the marinade and turning frequently, until lightly charred all over, about 10 minutes.

To make the dipping sauce, put all the ingredients in a blender and process until smooth. Transfer to six small bowls and serve alongside the kabobs.

tip: As an alternative to cooking on the grill, cook the kabobs on the stove top in a large, shallow skillet over high heat, brushing occasionally with the marinade and turning frequently, until lightly charred all over, about 10 minutes. Your kitchen may get a little smoky, but if you can stand it, cooking over high heat is the way to get that charcoal-grilled barbecue taste.

Sweet-and-Sour Tofu

The key to making this dish is slowly simmering the sauce for more than an hour. During that time, wonderful things will happen to the pineapple and cider vinegar, I assure you. Be patient, and the sauce will envelop the tofu and bok choy in sweet-and-sour perfection.

6 cups (1.5 L) pineapple chunks

4 cups (1 L) pineapple juice

2 green bell peppers, diced

2 red bell peppers, diced

2 onions, diced

6 ounces (170 g) no-salt-added tomato paste

1 cup (250 ml) cider vinegar

¾ cup (185 ml) granulated sugar

1½ pounds (680 g) firm tofu, cut into ¾-inch (2 cm) cubes

¼ cup (60 ml) water

1 tablespoon (15 ml) cornstarch

10 baby bok choy, sliced

Salt

Freshly ground black pepper

MAKES 6 SERVINGS

Per serving:
564 calories
24 g protein
12 g fat (0 g sat)
94 g carbohydrates
712 mg sodium
424 mg calcium
8 g fiber

Note: Analysis does not include salt and freshly ground black pepper to taste.

Put the pineapple, pineapple juice, green bell peppers, red bell peppers, onions, tomato paste, vinegar, and sugar in a large saucepan. Bring to a boil over medium-high heat, stirring occasionally. Decrease the heat to low, cover, and cook, stirring occasionally, for 70 minutes. Add the tofu and cook, stirring occasionally, for 25 minutes.

Put the water and cornstarch in a small bowl and stir until the cornstarch dissolves. Add the cornstarch mixture to the pan and stir to combine. Add the bok choy and cook, stirring occasionally, until the bok choy is tender-crisp, about 5 minutes. Season with salt and pepper to taste.

SERVING SUGGESTION: Serve over hot steamed rice.

Old Salt (and Pepper) Tofu

An "old salt" is an experienced sailor, someone who has traveled the world's oceans and returned with salty (and no doubt peppery) tales to tell. This dish honors the old-timers but pleases the palates of all who enjoy a hearty and savory dinner.

2 pounds (900 g) firm tofu

1 cup (250 ml) unbleached all-purpose flour

¼ cup (60 ml) raw sesame seeds

¼ cup (60 ml) nutritional yeast flakes

1 teaspoon (5 ml) salt

1 teaspoon (5 ml) freshly ground black pepper

¼ cup (60 ml) vegetable oil, plus more if needed

2 tablespoons (30 ml) reduced-sodium tamari, plus more if desired (optional)

MAKES 5 SERVINGS

Per serving:

403 calories

29 g protein

22 g fat (6 g sat)

25 g carbohydrates

470 mg sodium

292 mg calcium

3 g fiber

Drain the tofu and wrap it in an absorbent towel for 10 minutes to absorb the excess moisture. Cut into cubes and put in a large bowl.

Put the flour, sesame seeds, nutritional yeast, salt, and pepper in a small bowl and stir until well combined. Add the flour mixture to the tofu, tossing gently with a rubber spatula until the tofu is well coated.

Heat 2 tablespoons (30 ml) of the oil in a large skillet over medium-high heat. When the oil is hot, add half the tofu and cook, stirring occasionally, until golden brown, 5 to 10 minutes. Add up to 1 tablespoon (15 ml) of additional oil, 1 teaspoon (5 ml) at a time, if needed to keep the tofu from sticking to the skillet. If a bolder flavor is desired, stir in half the optional tamari during the last minute of cooking. Repeat with the remaining oil, tofu, and optional tamari.

SERVING SUGGESTION: Serve the tofu over hot steamed rice and top it off with First Mate Mushroom and Kale Sauté (page 53).

Monodon monoceros

500 F

RÉPUBLIQUE DE DJIBOUTI

2013

Iceberg!

Nothing says "welcome to Antarctica" like the sighting of our first iceberg. In anticipation of this awe-inspiring moment, we often place bets to see who can guess the latitude that will bring us our first glimpse of big ice.

Some of the icebergs we see stretch for miles and miles and are hundreds of feet high. It's mind-blowing to think that we're seeing only the top one-third of the berg and that the remaining two-thirds is underwater. Icebergs come in all shapes and sizes, some with arches and caves, others with cracks and crevices. And when they become top-heavy, they flip over and radiate an intense iridescent blue.

I'm a fan of the smaller icebergs, the ones that are low enough to allow penguins to climb on and take sanctuary from the hungry leopard seals. The small Arctic, or Adélie, penguin is the most common species of penguin that we come across in Antarctica. They are fairly short and have such shameless curiosity; they'll circle around you and simply stare if given the chance. I never tire of watching them lead their busy, dangerous, and very social lives. Although they appear hopelessly uncoordinated on the ice as they waddle, stumble, and slip around, in the water they're as graceful as any seal or whale. Groups can often be seen swimming swiftly in unison, skimming the surface and showing off their graceful version of the butterfly stroke.

Bob Barker Yum Bowls

This legendary recipe comes straight from the galley of the *Bob Barker*, the second vessel in our Sea Shepherd fleet. The heart of this dish is the Yum Sauce. Feel free to switch up the other ingredients in the bowls. We like ours hearty and usually include rice, potatoes, and beans.

YUM SAUCE (Makes 3 cups/750 ml)

½ cup (125 ml) water

½ cup (125 ml) silken tofu

½ cup (125 ml) vegetable oil

½ cup (125 ml) raw almonds

¼ cup (60 ml) no-salt-added cooked or canned chickpeas, rinsed and drained

¼ cup (60 ml) nutritional yeast flakes

¼ cup (60 ml) freshly squeezed lemon juice

2 cloves garlic

½ teaspoon (2 ml) dried oregano

½ teaspoon (2 ml) ground coriander

½ teaspoon (2 ml) curry powder

½ teaspoon (2 ml) salt

FOR THE BOWLS

3 cups (750 ml) hot cooked brown rice

2 potatoes, cubed and roasted

2 cups (500 ml) no-salt-added cooked or canned black beans, drained and rinsed

1½ cups (375 ml) sweet corn kernels

3 tomatoes, diced

1 avocado, sliced

Salt

Freshly ground black pepper

To make the sauce, put all the ingredients in a blender and process until smooth.

To assemble the bowls, divide the rice equally among six serving bowls. Top with equal portions of the potatoes, beans, corn, tomatoes, and avocado. Season with salt and pepper to taste. Top each bowl with ½ cup (125 ml) of Yum Sauce.

MAKES 6 SERVINGS

Per serving:

582 calories

16 g protein

30 g fat (7 g sat)

65 g carbohydrates

202 mg sodium

94 mg calcium

13 g fiber

Note: Analysis does not include salt and freshly ground black pepper to taste.

Chunky Beef, Barley, and Ale Stew

A hearty winter, pub-grub meal, this rich stew will satisfy even the biggest appetites. It's a treasure trove of veggies, beans, barley, and even vegan beef.

8 cups (2 L) diced tomatoes

6 cloves garlic, peeled

1½ tablespoons (22 ml) vegetable oil

1 teaspoon (5 ml) salt

1 teaspoon (5 ml) freshly ground black pepper, plus more as needed

3 tablespoons (45 ml) coconut oil

1 onion, diced

1 zucchini, diced

1 cup (250 ml) diced celery

1½ tablespoons (22 ml) reduced-sodium tamari

1½ cups (375 ml) vegan beef-style chunks

2½ cups (625 ml) peeled and diced pumpkin

2 cups (500 ml) no-salt-added vegan beef-style broth

2 cups (500 ml) peeled and diced potatoes

1 cup (250 ml) no-salt-added cooked or canned kidney beans, rinsed and drained

½ cup (125 ml) pearled barley

1 teaspoon (5 ml) crushed red chile flakes

1 teaspoon (5 ml) rubbed sage

1 bay leaf

1 bottle (12 ounces/375 ml) stout

MAKES 6 SERVINGS

Per serving:
420 calories
11 g protein
15 g fat (2 g sat)
45 g carbohydrates
832 mg sodium
158 mg calcium
103 g fiber

Preheat the oven to 350 degrees F (180 degrees C).

Put the tomatoes and garlic on a rimmed baking sheet and sprinkle with the vegetable oil, salt, and pepper. Bake until the tomatoes and garlic are soft and fragrant, about 30 minutes.

While the tomatoes are baking, heat the coconut oil in a large soup pot over medium heat. Add the onion, zucchini, celery, tamari, and a pinch of pepper and cook until the onion is soft and translucent, about 10 minutes. Add the beef-style chunks and cook until golden brown, about 10 minutes.

Transfer the tomatoes and garlic and their juices to the soup pot. Add the pumpkin, broth, potatoes, beans, barley, chile flakes, sage, and bay leaf and stir to combine. Increase the heat to medium-high and bring to a boil. Decrease the heat to medium, cover, and cook, stirring occasionally, until the potatoes and barley are tender, about 40 minutes. Add the stout and stir until well incorporated. Remove the bay leaf before serving.

SERVING SUGGESTION: Serve in deep soup bowls with thick slices of crusty bread.

Chickpea Curry for a Courageous Crew

I was taking a cooking class in India when I got the most valuable advice for making curry: always grind your own spices. I got hold of a mortar and pestle as soon as I returned to the galley, and I have used it almost every day since. The fragrance and taste of freshly ground coriander seeds, cumin seeds, and peppercorns really do make all the difference.

2 tablespoons (30 ml) vegetable oil

2 onions, diced

1 piece (2½ inches/6 cm) ginger, peeled and finely minced

2 Thai chiles, seeded and thinly sliced

1 tablespoon (15 ml) cumin seeds, lightly crushed

2 cloves garlic, minced

2 teaspoons (10 ml) coriander seeds, ground

1 teaspoon (5 ml) ground turmeric

1 teaspoon (5 ml) paprika

2½ cups (625 ml) no-salt-added cooked or canned chickpeas, rinsed and drained

1½ cups (375 ml) no-salt-added vegetable broth

Heat the oil in a large soup pot over medium-high heat. Add the onions, ginger, chiles, cumin, and garlic and cook, stirring frequently, until the onions begin to brown, about 15 minutes. Add the coriander, turmeric, and paprika and cook, stirring frequently to prevent the spices from burning, for 5 minutes. Decrease the heat to medium. Add the chickpeas and broth and cook, stirring occasionally, until most of the liquid has evaporated, about 10 minutes.

SERVING SUGGESTION: Serve over hot steamed basmati rice.

MAKES 4 SERVINGS

Per serving:

232 calories

7 g protein

9 g fat (2 g sat)

31 g carbohydrates

13 mg sodium

6 mg calcium

5 g fiber

Fish-Free Cakes

The best thing about these fish cakes is, of course, that they're not made of fish. The addition of nori, a sea vegetable, and vegan fish sauce gives them the taste of the ocean.

1 sheet nori, cut into thin, short strips

1¾ cups (435 ml) no-salt-added cooked or canned chickpeas, rinsed, drained, and finely chopped

¼ cup (60 ml) vegetable oil, plus more for the skillet

1 medium potato, peeled, cooked, and mashed

3 ounces (85 g) firm tofu, mashed

¼ red onion, minced

2 tablespoons (30 ml) vegan fish sauce

1 tablespoon (15 ml) tapioca starch or potato starch, plus more as needed

1 tablespoon (15 ml) nutritional yeast flakes

1 teaspoon (5 ml) salt

1 cup (250 ml) bread crumbs or potato flour

MAKES 8 FISH-FREE CAKES

Per fish-free cake:

170 calories

5 g protein

9 g fat (2 g sat)

16 g carbohydrates

326 mg sodium

37 mg calcium

2 g fiber

Note: Analysis does not include extra tapioca starch, if needed.

Put the nori in a large bowl. Add the chickpeas and oil and stir until well combined. (The oil will help prevent the nori from clumping as it tends to do when wet; avoid clumping as much as possible.) Add the potato, tofu, onion, fish sauce, tapioca starch, nutritional yeast, and salt and mix with your hands until well combined. The mixture should be cohesive enough to form firm patties. If the mixture doesn't hold together, add up to 1 tablespoon (15 ml) of additional starch, 1 teaspoon (5 ml) at a time, until it does.

Put the bread crumbs on a large plate. Divide the chickpea mixture into eight equal portions and press each into a small patty using your hands. Press both sides of each patty into the bread crumbs and transfer to a large plate.

Line a large plate with paper towels. Oil a large skillet and heat over medium heat. Carefully put the fish cakes in the skillet; the oil may splatter, so take care that you don't get burned. Cook on each side until deep golden brown, about 7 minutes per side. Transfer to the lined plate to remove any excess oil. You may need to cook the patties in two or three batches, depending on the size of your skillet.

SERVING SUGGESTION: These patties can be served sandwich-style or on a plate with a side of brown rice. Either way, they're great accented with a squeeze or two of fresh lemon or with tartar sauce. To make vegan tartar sauce, combine Creamy Dill Mayonnaise (page 113) with minced dill pickles to taste. It's as easy as that!

Brazilian Beans with Tomato-Orange Salsa

Together, these beans and salsa are one class (or classic) act. The beans themselves are extraordinarily versatile and can be used so many ways. For example, combine them with cooked rice for a traditional version of beans and rice, add them to a burrito, or slather them over toast for a filling breakfast.

BRAZILIAN BEANS

3 tablespoons (45 ml) olive oil

8 cloves garlic, minced

1 onion, finely diced

Pinch freshly ground black pepper

15 cups (3.75 L) water

3 cups (750 ml) dried pinto beans, picked over, rinsed, and drained

2 teaspoons (20 ml) salt

1 bay leaf

TOMATO-ORANGE SALSA

3 tomatoes, finely diced (see tip)

2 oranges, seeded and finely diced (see tip)

¼ onion, very finely diced

½ cup (125 ml) coarsely chopped fresh cilantro

Pinch freshly ground black pepper

1 lime, sliced into 6 wedges

MAKES 6 SERVINGS

Per serving:
415 calories
21 g protein
9 g fat (1 g sat)
69 g carbohydrates
782 mg sodium
130 mg calcium
10 g fiber

To make the beans, put the oil and garlic in a large soup pot over low heat and cook, stirring almost constantly, until the garlic is golden brown, 5 to 8 minutes (the longer and slower the garlic cooks, the better). Add the onion and pepper and increase the heat to medium. Cook, stirring frequently, until the onion is soft and translucent, about 10 minutes. Add the water, beans, salt, and bay leaf and stir to combine. Cover and bring to a boil. Decrease the heat to medium-low. Partially cover and cook until the beans are tender, 40 to 45 minutes. Remove the bay leaf before serving.

To make the salsa, put the tomatoes, oranges, onion, cilantro, and pepper in a large bowl and toss to combine. Top each serving of beans with a dollop of salsa and a lime wedge.

tip: To retain their wonderful juices, be sure to use a sharp knife to cut the tomatoes and oranges for the salsa.

Dave's Misir Wat

Occasionally we have a guest star in the galley, when a member of the crew comes in and cooks a favorite recipe. What a cool way to learn new dishes. This interpretation of a traditional Ethiopian lentil dish comes from Dave Nickarz, self-appointed tenth engineer and longtime crew member.

2 tablespoons (30 ml) vegetable oil

1 onion, minced

3 tablespoons (45 ml) ground berbere

4 cloves garlic, minced

½ teaspoon (2 ml) ground cardamom

1 can (14.28 ounces/405 g) no-salt-added tomato purée

2½ cups (625 ml) dried red lentils, picked over, rinsed, and drained

5 cups (1.25 L) water, plus more as needed

Salt

Put the oil in a large soup pot over medium heat. When the oil is hot, add the onion and cook, stirring frequently, until it begins to brown, about 15 minutes. Add the berbere, garlic, and cardamom and cook, stirring frequently so the spices don't burn, for 5 minutes. Add the tomato purée and cook, stirring occasionally, for 10 minutes.

Add the lentils and stir to combine. Gradually add the water, about ½ cup (125 ml) at a time, and cook, stirring frequently, until all the water has been absorbed and the lentils are tender, 20 to 30 minutes. The dahl should be fairly thick. It will thicken further as it cools. If the dahl is too thin, cook it a little longer; if it is too thick, add a little more water to achieve the desired consistency. Season with salt to taste.

SERVING SUGGESTION: Serve over hot steamed rice.

MAKES 4 SERVINGS

Per serving:

568 calories

34 g protein

7 g fat (2 g sat)

89 g carbohydrates

38 mg sodium

101 mg calcium

24 g fiber

Note: Analysis does not include salt to taste.

Sailors' Delight Sausages

After a long quest to perfect the homemade vegan sausage, Priya (my galley buddy and partner in "Operation Relentless") came up with the ultimate recipe. These are so good, I'm often caught sneaking into the fridge at night to snack on the leftovers!

1¼ cups (310 ml) vital wheat gluten

1¼ cups (310 ml) nutritional yeast flakes

1 cup (250 ml) no-salt-added vegetable broth

½ cup (125 ml) no-salt-added cooked or canned beans (cannellini, kidney, or pinto), rinsed, drained, and mashed

2 tablespoons (30 ml) reduced-sodium tamari

1 tablespoon (15 ml) vegetable oil

1 teaspoon (5 ml) dried oregano

1 teaspoon (5 ml) garlic powder

1 teaspoon (5 ml) paprika

1 teaspoon (5 ml) freshly ground black pepper

½ teaspoon (2 ml) crushed red chile flakes

½ teaspoon (2 ml) dried thyme

MAKES ABOUT 15 SAUSAGES

Per sausage:
71 calories
10 g protein
1 g fat (0.3 g sat)
5 g carbohydrates
98 mg sodium
14 mg calcium
1 g fiber

Put all the ingredients in a large bowl and mix well, using your hands. Divide the mixture into fifteen equal portions and stretch and roll each portion into a sausage shape. Put on a large plate.

Wrap each sausage tightly in aluminum foil. Put the sausages in a steamer and cover. You will need to do this in batches, depending on the size of the steamer.

Steam each batch for 30 minutes, checking the water level after each batch and adding more water to the steamer if necessary.

Transfer the sausages to a large plate and let cool. Once the sausages are completely cool, lightly brown them in an oiled skillet over medium heat. Serve immediately. Alternatively, put the sausages in a tightly sealed container and store in the refrigerator, where they will keep for 5 days, or in the freezer, where they will keep for 3 months.

tip: Not to be confused with high-gluten flour, vital wheat gluten is made from the main protein of wheat and binds together the ingredients in this recipe.

SERVING SUGGESTION: Serve with Roasted Potato and Yam Medley (page 95) and a green salad.

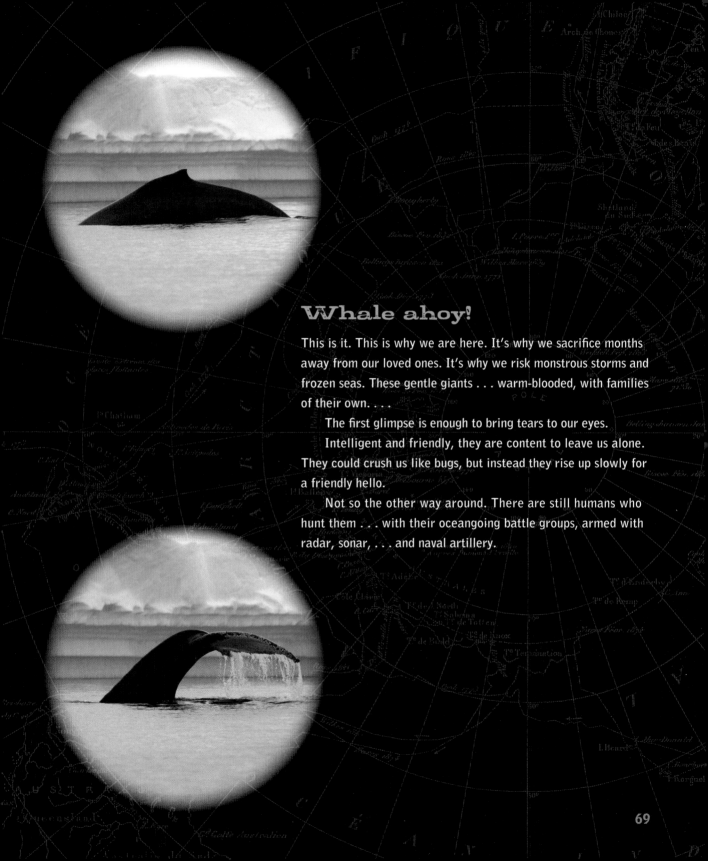

Whale ahoy!

This is it. This is why we are here. It's why we sacrifice months away from our loved ones. It's why we risk monstrous storms and frozen seas. These gentle giants . . . warm-blooded, with families of their own. . . .

The first glimpse is enough to bring tears to our eyes.

Intelligent and friendly, they are content to leave us alone. They could crush us like bugs, but instead they rise up slowly for a friendly hello.

Not so the other way around. There are still humans who hunt them . . . with their oceangoing battle groups, armed with radar, sonar, . . . and naval artillery.

69

Rockin' the Boat Risotto

Risotto will give your stirring arm a workout, but the resulting creaminess will be worth it—and leave you and everyone else fighting for second helpings! The fresh basil and chives, which are added at the end, give this dish an extra kick of flavor.

¼ cup (60 ml) vegan butter

20 button mushrooms, thinly sliced

1 onion, diced

1 teaspoon (5 ml) freshly ground black pepper

7 cups (1.75 L) no-salt-added vegan chicken-style broth

3½ cups (875 ml) arborio rice

¾ cup (185 ml) dry white wine

1 cup (250 ml) fresh or thawed frozen green peas

¼ cup (60 ml) fresh basil leaves, packed

1 tablespoon (15 ml) thinly sliced fresh chives

Put the butter in a large soup pot over medium-high heat. When the butter is melted, add the mushrooms, onion, and pepper and cook until the onion is soft and translucent, about 10 minutes. Add the rice and 3½ cups (875 ml) of the broth, stirring constantly. Decrease the heat to low, cover, and bring to a gentle simmer. Uncover and cook until all the liquid has evaporated. Gradually stir in the remaining 3½ cups (875 ml) of broth and the wine, ½ cup at a time. Cook, stirring constantly, until the liquid is almost completely absorbed.

Remove from the heat. Add the peas, basil, and chives and stir until evenly distributed. Serve immediately.

MAKES 6 SERVINGS

Per serving:

565 calories

12 g protein

7 g fat (2 g sat)

103 g carbohydrates

113 mg sodium

0 mg calcium

4 g fiber

300 F
Physeter macrocephalus
RÉPUBLIQUE DE DJIBOUTI
2013

Taste-of-the-Sea Spaghetti

Nori, a nutrition-rich sea vegetable, imparts a subtle flavor and adds an interesting twist to classic spaghetti with red sauce. Don't be alarmed by the large quantity of garlic called for in this recipe. Slow cooking removes the sting, leaving a deep robust flavor that seafarers just can't get enough of!

½ cup (125 ml) olive oil

10 cloves garlic, minced

3 red onions, finely diced

6 sheets nori, cut into thin, short strips

2 large tomatoes, diced

2 teaspoons (10 ml) reduced-sodium tamari

1 teaspoon (5 ml) freshly ground black pepper

2 pounds (900 g) spaghetti

6 tablespoons (90 ml) nutritional yeast flakes

MAKES 6 SERVINGS

Per serving:
750 calories
23 g protein
20 g fat (1 g sat)
121 g carbohydrates
85 mg sodium
47 mg calcium
9 g fiber

Put the oil and garlic in a large, deep skillet or saucepan over low heat and cook, stirring almost constantly, until the garlic is golden brown, 5 to 8 minutes (the longer and slower the garlic cooks, the better). Add the onions and nori and increase the heat to medium. Cook, stirring frequently, until the onions are soft and translucent, about 10 minutes. Decrease the heat to low. Add the tomatoes, tamari, and pepper and cook, stirring occasionally, for 30 minutes.

While the sauce cooks, prepare the spaghetti according to the package instructions. Drain and transfer to a large serving bowl. Top with the sauce, sprinkle with the nutritional yeast, and toss until evenly distributed.

Q&A
WITH CAPTAIN PAUL

Captain Paul Watson is one of the founders of the radical environmental movement. He also founded the Sea Shepherd Conservation Society, which has grown exponentially over the past thirty-five years. Today Sea Shepherd is active in thirty-six countries and has hundreds of thousands of supporters and members. Captain Paul commands the four large vessels in the Sea Shepherd anti-poaching fleet—the flagship *Steve Irwin*, the *Bob Barker*, the *Brigitte Bardot*, and the *Sam Simon*—and also oversees numerous smaller, faster boats. The fleet campaigns worldwide and makes an aggressive, direct-action approach for the protection of all threatened marine wildlife.

If the fish die off, the ocean dies. And if the ocean dies, we die.

Sea Shepherd is unique among environmental organizations in that its founder continues to take the helm and lead from the front. But Paul is not only our captain—he's also a fantastic chef! Sometimes he comes into the galley to make the crew one of his delicious dishes, such as Captain's Habitat Split Pea Soup (page 34) or Antarctic Tropical Canadian Delight (page 143).

On the following pages are some questions Captain Paul

LAURA: Paul, in your opinion, is there such a thing as sustainable fishing and aquaculture, or should seafood be left off the menu altogether?

CAPTAIN PAUL: I was raised in a village in eastern Canada, where the villagers fished for lobster. So since childhood I've seen the diversity in our ocean diminish steadily. Fishery after fishery has collapsed. There are simply not enough fish in the sea to meet the excessive demands of the ever-expanding human population. Rather than being served on our plates, fish must be allowed to play the more important role of maintaining the ecological stability and integrity of the sea.

LAURA: How does overfishing and the depletion of the oceans directly affect the environment?

CAPTAIN PAUL: The strength of any ecosystem is diversity. With diminished diversity and diminished interdependence between species, an ecosystem will collapse and will die. If the fish die off, the ocean dies. And if the ocean dies, we die.

LAURA: How did you learn to cook?

CAPTAIN PAUL: My father was a chef, and I left home when I was fifteen and had to fend for myself. Cooking is a survival art. In fact, Antarctic explorer Ernest Shackleton's first question to expedition volunteers was to ask them if they could cook. If they said no, he rejected them. His opinion was that if a man couldn't cook for himself, he was essentially useless as an explorer.

LAURA: What is your favorite dish to prepare?

CAPTAIN PAUL: I like preparing soups, especially pea, tomato, and mushroom soups.

LAURA: What food can't you stand?

CAPTAIN PAUL: I've had a lifelong aversion to sweet potatoes, and I'm not a fan of chocolate.

LAURA: What is your favorite cuisine?

CAPTAIN PAUL: Thai, followed by Chinese. I also like Greek.

LAURA: Can you give a brief history of the ships' galleys?

CAPTAIN PAUL: We began our campaigns in 1978 with the *Sea Shepherd,* and the galley served only vegetarian food. Since 2005, only vegan food has been served on the ships.

LAURA: Although Sea Shepherd is not an animals rights organization, and crew members are not required to be vegan, why did you decide it was important for the galleys to serve vegan food?

CAPTAIN PAUL: People are eating our oceans to death. No fish is safe. What most people don't realize, however, is that meat eating also greatly diminishes the oceans, because 40 percent of the fish taken from the sea is fed to pigs, chickens, cows, domestic cats, and farm-raised fish. In fact, pigs are eating more fish than sharks, chickens are eating more fish than puffins, and cats are eating more fish than seals. So really, when you eat bacon, you're eating the sea. By serving only vegan food, we illustrate the relationship between what we eat and the health of our oceans.

LAURA: Why is food so important on the vessels and to the crew?

CAPTAIN PAUL: On all ships, mealtime is an important time of day for crew members. If the crew is well fed, they're happy, and when they're happy, they do their best.

LAURA: What is the most amazing sight you have witnessed during your many years at sea?

CAPTAIN PAUL: In 1975, I was swimming in one of the many small straits of Bella Bella, British Columbia. I was in the path of an oncoming pod of orcas. It was an intimidating sight, seeing them approach. I mean, these guys eat sea lions. And as they passed, I grabbed the dorsal fin of one and actually rode her for about two hundred meters before tumbling back into her wake. All I could think was here was this powerful animal, the strongest predator in the animal world, and she allowed me to ride on her back. It was an amazing insight into the nature of this magnificent creature.

LAURA: Why are whales still hunted and killed?

CAPTAIN PAUL: The primary market is in Japan, although whale meat provides less than 1 percent of the protein consumed in that country. Iceland kills whales for the Japanese market. Norway is the only other country where people include whales in their diet. The Faroese, residents of Denmark's Faroe Islands, kill whales for sport. The Japanese kill whales when they capture dolphins for aquariums.

LAURA: Why did you decide to take on marine conservation over other issues?

CAPTAIN PAUL: I started defending beavers by releasing them from leghold traps when I was ten years old, and I have worked with elephants in Africa and wolves in the Yukon. But my experience working on ships in the merchant marine and in the coast guard gave me the skills to go to sea, and I decided in 1979 to devote myself to protecting marine life.

LAURA: Although a lot of people find direct action (for example, ramming poaching vessels) controversial, why is it important? And how is it effective?

CAPTAIN PAUL: Direct action gives us results and saves lives. It also provides drama, which captures the public's attention, so it's both effective and educational.

LAURA: What is your favorite time of day on the ship?

CAPTAIN PAUL: I like to watch the sunrise and the sunset.

LAURA: Do you have any galley stories you want to share with folks?

CAPTAIN PAUL: The ship was anchored in Cannes and I was in the galley talking with a crew member when a couple of women who were touring the ship came in. One of the women asked me how she could join the crew. Not recognizing her, I answered that she should get a crew application online and send it in. As I left the galley, the crew member followed me and said, "You know, that woman is Michelle Rodriguez, the actress who played the helicopter pilot in the film *Avatar*." I turned and went back into the galley and said, "On second thought, forget the application, we do need a kick-ass helicopter pilot. When can you join?" She joined the crew later that year, but not as a helicopter pilot. Turns out she was a damn good small-boat operator.

78

SALADS AND SIDES

Salads and sides make up a large and important part of our meals. Because the crew has little to no control over what they eat and when, we feel it's important to give them as much choice as possible. We do this by offering a variety of different side dishes they can choose from.

Greek Sailor Salad

This salad is beautiful, colorful, and crunchy. With its intense combination of flavors, it can be the life of the party—and it's almost a meal in itself. It's a delight to have on board.

1 head cos lettuce, sliced

3 tomatoes, diced

2 green bell peppers, diced

2 red bell peppers, diced

½ red onion, thinly sliced

½ cup (125 ml) pitted kalamata olives

1 cup (250 ml) Savory Tofu Feta (page 114) and 2 tablespoons (30 ml) of the marinade

Salt

Freshly ground black pepper

MAKES 4 SERVINGS

Per serving:

329 calories

18 g protein

21 g fat (3 g sat)

22 g carbohydrates

425 mg sodium

203 mg calcium

7 g fiber

Note: Analysis does not include salt and freshly ground black pepper to taste.

Put the lettuce, tomatoes, green bell peppers, red bell peppers, onion, and olives in a large salad bowl. Top with the Tofu Feta and marinade and toss until the vegetables are evenly coated with the marinade. Season with salt and pepper to taste. Serve immediately, while the lettuce is crisp.

Below-Sea-Level Salad

Our take on the popular Israeli salad, this fresh side becomes our everyday salad when we have been at sea for a while, as it combines a number of longer-lasting fruits and vegetables. Purchased unripened, tomatoes can keep for forty days at sea. Cucumbers don't hold up quite as long, unfortunately.

¼ head Chinese cabbage, finely chopped
3 tomatoes, finely diced
2 cucumbers, finely diced
1 green bell pepper, finely diced
¼ red onion, finely diced
Juice of 1 lemon
1 tablespoon (15 ml) olive oil
Salt
Freshly ground black pepper

Put the cabbage, tomatoes, cucumbers, bell pepper, onion, lemon juice, and oil in a medium salad bowl and toss well. Season with salt and pepper to taste and toss again.

SERVING SUGGESTION: This salad is an ideal complement to Middle Eastern or Indian dishes.

MAKES 4 SERVINGS

Per serving:

88 calories

3 g protein

4 g fat (1 g sat)

13 g carbohydrates

42 mg sodium

80 mg calcium

3 g fiber

Note: Analysis does not include salt and freshly ground black pepper to taste.

Easterly Edamame Salad

If you're not on a ship, this is an ideal salad to take to a picnic in the park. It can last out of the fridge for several hours, providing it's not in direct sunlight, and will remain a vibrant green. Ideally, let the edamame soak in the dressing for a few hours so it can absorb all the Eastern-inspired flavors.

½ red onion, minced

1½ sheets nori, cut into thin, short strips

2 tablespoons (30 ml) raw sesame seeds

2 cloves garlic, crushed

1 tablespoon (15 ml) peeled and minced fresh ginger

1 tablespoon (15 ml) toasted sesame oil

1 tablespoon (15 ml) rice vinegar

2 teaspoons (10 ml) reduced-sodium tamari

1½ pounds (680 grams) frozen edamame, cooked according to the package instructions

MAKES 6 SERVINGS

Per serving:

193 calories

13 g protein

9 g fat (2 g sat)

18 g carbohydrates

137 mg sodium

87 mg calcium

8 g fiber

Put the onion, nori, sesame seeds, garlic, ginger, oil, vinegar, and tamari in a large bowl and stir until well combined. Add the edamame and stir until evenly coated.

Cover and let sit for 10 minutes to allow the flavors to meld. Stir, cover, and let sit for 10 minutes longer before serving.

Boatload of Butternut Caponata

This hearty caponata descends from a traditional Italian sailor's dish. This version is a lot like a mild salsa, and it's extraordinarily versatile. Enjoy it warm or cold, as an accompaniment to hot dishes or stuffed into a sandwich.

10 large tomatoes, quartered

2 cloves garlic, peeled

¼ cup (60 ml) olive oil

2 teaspoons (10 ml) dried basil

1 teaspoon (5 ml) dried rosemary

1 teaspoon (5 ml) salt, plus more as needed

1 teaspoon (5 ml) freshly ground black pepper, plus more as needed

½ teaspoon (2 ml) rubbed sage

1 medium butternut squash, peeled and cubed

1 green bell pepper, cut into 8 pieces

1 red bell pepper, cut into 8 pieces

1 yellow bell pepper, cut into 8 pieces

Preheat the oven to 300 degrees F (150 degrees C).

Put the tomatoes and whole garlic cloves on a rimmed baking sheet. Put 2 tablespoons (30 ml) of the oil and the basil, rosemary, salt, pepper, and sage in a small bowl and stir to combine. Pour evenly over the tomatoes and garlic. Bake for 1 hour. Transfer to a large serving bowl and set aside.

Increase the oven temperature to 425 degrees F (220 degrees C). Put the squash, green bell peppers, red bell peppers, and yellow bell peppers on the baking sheet and sprinkle evenly with the remaining 2 tablespoons (30 ml) of oil and a pinch of salt and pepper. Bake for 20 minutes, or until the edges of the bell peppers begin to brown.

Transfer to the bowl with the tomatoes and stir to combine. Serve warm or at room temperature. Stored in a sealed container in the refrigerator, Boatload of Butternut Caponata will keep for 3 weeks.

MAKES 6 SERVINGS

Per serving:

183 calories

4 g protein

10 g fat (1 g sat)

24 g carbohydrates

399 mg sodium

45 mg calcium

6 g fiber

Malcolm Holland, SAILING MASTER, *STEVE IRWIN*

Ten days had passed since our scout vessel had been smashed in two. The salvage operation had cost dear time and allowed the factory whaling ship to make a run for the far western end of the whaling grounds. Three barbarous kill ships ran with it.

In the hours that had just passed, signs that the death ships were near had tallied steadily. The atmosphere on our vessel was one of quiet and intent focus. The crew's determination amplified as we sat in radio silence, enshrouded in a cloud of white sea mist, breathing in the cleanest air on earth.

Deckhand Darius was harnessed to the top of the black foremast. As the mist cleared and the ocean revealed itself in mirror gray, he lowered his binoculars and signed back to the wheelhouse. There was something up ahead, beyond the dip of hard horizon.

Ice of many shapes and every scale drifted in this bay. However, it could not conceal the mast configuration of the industrial whaling factory ship that emerged from the mist. Although we surged forward, the ship seemingly remained distant and evasive. With gloved hands, we shifted and steadied our binoculars, keeping it in view.

Lying motionless in immaculate white polar night, the vessel was, so far, unaffected by our presence. But what if this was not our target? Suppose we emerged from the fog in the presence of a ship other than the one we hunted—a toothfish poacher, perhaps, or a marauding krill trawler. I joined Darius on the foremast.

Verification, however, was a formality—a mere excuse for a watchkeeper to do something physical before the coming hours of concentration. Right ahead was the flagship of Kyodo Senpaku, the corporation that pedals whale parts while operating under the guise of "research."

Back in the wheelhouse, the notification went out to the engine room and galley. We made our move, bringing the whale defense ship around to head for a place near the bow of the factory ship. The engines and propeller were pushed to the max. Autopilot was switched off and the helm controlled by hand. Unnecessary and inefficient rudder movements were minimized to make good the surprise while it was ours.

Minutes later, the factory ship made its move too. New smoke blackened the Antarctic sky. From our perspective, the *Nisshin's* longitudinal profile became A-frame. Creating a turbulent wake, the factory ship turned to the north in a bid to exit the killing grounds and enter the subpolar storm belt. The chase was on.

In the hours to come, attendant kill ships would be with us, and with them would come new challenges. For now though, the killers were on the run. Crew members moved to their action stations.

Already, I could smell the Hot Chile Chocolate (page 144) that was simmering in the galley, the vegan heart of our vessel, in advance of our traditional celebration. Nothing could keep my joy from rising and releasing itself as a grin. In that moment, our brave crew could scarcely have done more in its struggle for a world free from domination.

AN 8,000-TON FACTORY SHIP

AGAINST A 40-TON WHALE?
THAT DOESN'T SEEM FAIR.

丸新日
NISSHIN MARU

WHY NOT PICK ON SOMEONE YOUR OWN SIZE?

Asian-Style Stuffed Dumplings

These dumplings are definitely worth the effort! Stuffing dumplings is an art form, so don't beat yourself up if yours come out kind of wonky the first time. With practice, you'll nail it.

FILLING

1 tablespoon (15 ml) toasted sesame oil, plus more for brushing the dumplings

2 carrots, scrubbed (peeling optional) and grated

½ cup (125 ml) finely chopped shiitake mushrooms

3 green onions, sliced

1 piece (2 inches/5 cm) ginger, peeled and minced

1 tablespoon (15 ml) minced garlic

2 tablespoons (30 ml) raw sesame seeds

2 tablespoons (30 ml) reduced-sodium tamari

2 tablespoons (30 ml) sweet soy sauce

DOUGH

1½ cups (375 ml) warm water

2 tablespoons (30 ml) granulated sugar

2 teaspoons (10 ml) active dry yeast

3 cups (750 ml) unbleached all-purpose flour, plus more for rolling the dough

½ teaspoon (2 ml) salt

1 tablespoon (15 ml) vegetable oil

MAKES 10 DUMPLINGS

Per dumpling:
198 calories
5 g protein
4 g fat (2 g sat)
35 g carbohydrates
393 mg sodium
3 mg calcium
2 g fiber

To make the filling, heat the toasted sesame oil in a large skillet over medium-high heat. When the oil is hot, add the carrots, mushrooms, green onions, ginger, and garlic and cook, stirring frequently, until the vegetables are soft, about 15 minutes. Add the sesame seeds, tamari, and sweet soy sauce and cook, stirring occasionally, for 10 minutes. Remove from the heat and let cool.

To make the dough, put the water, sugar, and yeast in a small bowl, cover with a towel, and let sit in a warm spot until the mixture begins to froth, 5 to 10 minutes.

Put the flour and salt in a large bowl. Add the yeast mixture and vegetable oil and stir with a wooden spoon until a dough starts to form. Transfer the dough to a well-floured surface and knead for 10 minutes. Put the dough in a clean, oiled bowl (preferably wooden) and cover with a damp towel. Let sit in a warm place out of direct sunlight until doubled in size, about 1½ hours.

Preheat the oven to 375 degrees F (190 degrees C). Line a rimmed baking sheet with parchment paper.

Oil a large plate. Punch down the dough and knead it in the bowl for 1 to 2 minutes. Divide the dough into ten equal pieces and use your hands to roll each piece into a ball. Put the balls in a single layer on the oiled plate.

Put one ball of dough on a well-floured surface and roll it into a flat disk, about 4½ inches (11 cm) in diameter. Transfer to the lined baking sheet and spoon ¼ cup (60 ml) of filling into the center. Gather up the edges of the dough and bring them together at the top (like a drawstring purse). Press the edges together to create a secure seal. Repeat with the remaining dough and filling.

Brush the dumplings with toasted sesame oil and bake for 20 minutes, or until golden brown. Alternatively, steam in a steamer for 15 minutes.

Mediterranean Baked Tofu

Baked tofu is a healthy alternative to fried. Seasoned with plenty of garlic and basil, this rendition can transport a sailor right to the Mediterranean.

2 pounds (900 g) firm tofu, cubed

1/3 cup (85 ml) olive oil

1/4 cup (60 ml) cider vinegar

3 tablespoons (45 ml) nutritional yeast flakes

3 cloves garlic, sliced

1 tablespoon (15 ml) dried oregano

1 tablespoon (15 ml) reduced-sodium tamari

1 teaspoon (5 ml) salt

1/2 teaspoon (2 ml) freshly ground black pepper

1/2 cup (125 ml) coarsely chopped fresh basil, lightly packed

MAKES 6 SERVINGS

Per serving:
294 calories
18 g protein
22 g fat (3 g sat)
5 g carbohydrates
500 mg sodium
154 mg calcium
3 g fiber

Preheat the oven to 350 degrees F (180 degrees C). Line a baking sheet with parchment paper.

Arrange the tofu in a single layer on the lined baking sheet.

Put the oil, vinegar, nutritional yeast, garlic, oregano, tamari, salt, and pepper in a small bowl and stir until well combined. Gently stir in the basil. Spoon over the tofu and toss gently until the the tofu is well coated. Spread the tofu back into a single layer.

Bake for 15 minutes. Remove from the oven and flip the tofu with a metal spatula. Bake for about 15 minutes longer, until lightly crisp. Let cool slightly on the baking sheet. Transfer to a serving dish and top the tofu with any oil and herbs that remain on the baking sheet.

SERVING SUGGESTION: Serve with a green salad and a slice of crusty bread, which is handy for soaking up the oil and herbs, or use the tofu as a sandwich filling.

Spicy Fired-Up Potatoes

If you're looking to spice up a meal, these fiery potatoes will do the job. This side dish is a favorite any time of year, but it's an especially welcome addition to the table on cold days.

7 medium potatoes, scrubbed and cut into wedges

½ cup (125 ml) no-salt-added vegetable broth

2 tablespoons (30 ml) vegetable oil

1½ teaspoons (7 ml) minced fresh mixed herbs (dill weed, rosemary, thyme), or ½ teaspoon (2 ml) dried

1 teaspoon (5 ml) crushed red chile flakes

1 teaspoon (5 ml) salt

½ teaspoon (2 ml) freshly ground black pepper

Preheat the oven to 400 degrees F (205 degrees C). Line a rimmed baking sheet with parchment paper.

Arrange the potatoes in a single layer on the lined baking sheet.

Put the broth, oil, herbs, chile flakes, salt, and pepper in a small bowl and stir until well combined. Spoon the broth mixture evenly over the potatoes until well coated.

Bake for 20 minutes. Remove from the oven and flip the potatoes with a metal spatula. Bake for about 10 minutes longer, or until the liquid has evaporated and the potatoes have begun to crisp. Remove from the oven and flip the potatoes again. Bake for about 10 minutes longer, until crispy.

MAKES 4 SERVINGS

Per serving:

238 calories

7 g protein

7 g fat (2 g sat)

46 g carbohydrates

585 mg sodium

36 mg calcium

5 g fiber

Apple and Potato Oven Fries

In this twist on regular old roasted fries, apples and potatoes prove a surprisingly good combination. A squeeze of fresh lemon offsets the apples' sweetness just perfectly.

5 large potatoes, scrubbed (peeling optional) and cut into thick wedges
2 large, firm baking apples, peeled and cut into thick wedges
¼ cup (60 ml) olive oil
1 tablespoon (15 ml) minced fresh rosemary, or 1 teaspoon (5 ml) dried
Salt
Freshly ground black pepper
½ lemon, cut into small wedges

MAKES 6 SERVINGS

Per serving:
207 calories
3 g protein
9 g fat (1 g sat)
29 g carbohydrates
1 mg sodium
4 mg calcium
4 g fiber

Note: Analysis does not include salt and freshly ground black pepper to taste.

Preheat the oven to 400 degrees F (205 degrees C). Line a baking sheet with parchment paper.

Arrange the potatoes and apples in a single layer on the lined baking sheet. Sprinkle evenly with the oil and rosemary.

Bake for about 30 minutes, until the potatoes are fork-tender. Season with salt and pepper to taste. Transfer to a large serving bowl and garnish with the lemon wedges so diners can squeeze the lemon juice over their serving of fries as desired.

Roasted Potato and Yam Medley

Sweet potatoes are called a superfood because they're a concentrated source of nutrients as compared to many other vegetables. Here, the orange sweet potato and purple yam make a beautiful medley, packed full of vitamin A, vitamin C, and calcium.

1½ cups (375 ml) peeled and cubed potato

1 cup (250 ml) peeled and cubed orange sweet potato

1 cup (250 ml) peeled and cubed purple yam

1½ tablespoons (22 ml) vegetable oil

½ teaspoon (2 ml) dried dill weed

Pinch salt

Pinch freshly ground black pepper

¼ cup (60 ml) thinly sliced fresh chives

Preheat the oven to 400 degrees F (205 degrees C).

Put the potato, sweet potato, and yam in a 4-quart (4 L) baking dish. Sprinkle with the oil, dill weed, salt, and pepper and toss until the potatoes and yam are evenly coated.

Bake for 20 minutes and remove from the oven. Flip with a metal spatula and return to the oven. Bake for 25 to 30 minutes longer, or until tender and browned. Gently stir in the chives.

SERVING SUGGESTION: Serve as a side dish or as part of a tapas spread.

MAKES 4 SERVINGS

Per serving:

114 calories

2 g protein

5 g fat (2 g sat)

18 g carbohydrates

37 mg sodium

17 mg calcium

2 g fiber

Sweet Potatoes with Balsamic Onions

The balsamic onions in this dish offset the sweetness of the roasted sweet potatoes, creating a mouthwatering sweet-and-sour finish. Store any leftovers in the fridge; for a super-tasty way to use them up, stir them into hot pasta.

4 medium sweet potatoes, scrubbed and cut into 2-inch-thick slices
2 tablespoons (30 ml) vegetable oil
½ teaspoon (2 ml) salt
2 tablespoons (30 ml) olive oil
2 red onions, sliced
1 tablespoon (15 ml) dark brown sugar
½ teaspoon (2 ml) freshly ground black pepper
½ cup (125 ml) balsamic vinegar
2 cups (500 ml) stemmed baby spinach or arugula, packed

MAKES 4 SERVINGS

Per serving:
300 calories
4 g protein
14 g fat (3 g sat)
39 g carbohydrates
386 mg sodium
109 mg calcium
6 g fiber

Preheat the oven to 350 degrees F (180 degrees C). Line two rimmed baking sheets with parchment paper.

Arrange the sweet potatoes cut-side up on the lined baking sheets. Brush with the vegetable oil and sprinkle with the salt. Bake for 40 to 50 minutes, until fork-tender.

While the sweet potatoes bake, prepare the onions. Put the olive oil and onions in a skillet over medium-low heat and cook, stirring frequently, until the onions begin to caramelize, about 20 minutes. Sprinkle with the brown sugar and pepper and cook, stirring occasionally, until the onions are very soft and sweet, about 10 minutes longer. Remove from the heat and stir in the balsamic vinegar.

Transfer the sweet potatoes to a large serving dish. Spoon the onions evenly over the sweet potatoes. Top with the spinach. Let sit for 10 minutes before serving to allow the flavors to mingle.

SERVING SUGGESTION: For an attractive finishing touch, sprinkle some toasted pine nuts over the top before serving.

Admiral, there be whales here!
MONTGOMERY SCOTT

Far-from-Shore Tandoori Potatoes

On ship, our enthusiasm for potatoes never seems to wane. They keep well and can be prepared so many different ways. Here's one favorite, slightly exotic example, which vibrantly accompanies any Indian-themed meal.

⅓ cup (85 ml) vegetable oil
¼ cup (60 ml) nutritional yeast flakes
¼ cup (60 ml) tandoori paste
½ teaspoon (2 ml) freshly ground black pepper
5 large potatoes, scrubbed (peeling optional) and cubed
Salt
2 cups (500 ml) stemmed and coarsely chopped baby spinach, packed

Preheat the oven to 350 degrees F (180 degrees C). Line a rimmed baking sheet with parchment paper.

Put the oil, nutritional yeast, tandoori paste, and pepper in a large bowl and stir until well combined. Add the potatoes and stir until evenly coated.

Arrange the potatoes in a single layer on the lined baking sheet and bake for 25 minutes. Remove from the oven and flip with a metal spatula. Bake for about 20 minutes longer, until fork-tender.

Transfer the potatoes to a large serving bowl. Season with salt to taste. Add the spinach and toss gently until evenly distributed.

MAKES 6 SERVINGS

Per serving:
212 calories
5 g protein
12 g fat (4 g sat)
22 g carbohydrates
215 mg sodium
11 mg calcium
4 g fiber

Note: Analysis does not include salt to taste.

Megaptera novaeangliae
200 F
RÉPUBLIQUE DE DJIBOUTII
2013

SAUCES, SPREADS, AND CONDIMENTS

Whether on sea or land, we all crave flavor. And these are the recipes that provide it. In addition, legume- and seed-rich sauces and spreads are high in protein. So impart savory taste, a dab of extra nutrition, and compassion to your meals by accenting them with sauces, spreads, and condiments that contain no animal products.

Everyday Lemon-Tahini Sauce

We love this sauce and pour it over pretty much everything. As a bonus, tahini is an excellent source of calcium.

1 cup (250 ml) plain unsweetened nondairy milk
½ cup (125 ml) tahini
¼ cup (60 ml) olive oil
Juice of ½ lemon
1 tablespoon (15 ml) nutritional yeast flakes
1 tablespoon (15 ml) chopped fresh dill, or 1 teaspoon (5 ml) dried dill weed
1 tablespoon (15 ml) light miso
1 clove garlic

Put all the ingredients in a blender and process until smooth and creamy.

SERVING SUGGESTION: Incorporate the sauce into a hot entrée, such as a creamy baked pasta dish. Or thin the sauce with some cider vinegar to make a delicious salad dressing.

MAKES 2 CUPS (500 ML)

Per ¼ cup:
203 calories
5 g protein
19 g fat (2 g sat)
4 g carbohydrates
150 mg sodium
77 mg calcium
2 g fiber

Smooth-Sailing Peanut Sauce

Peanut sauce is wonderfully rich and creamy, not to mention packed with protein. And it's so easy to make: rarely will you get so much flavor for so little effort!

½ cup (125 ml) full-fat coconut milk

2 tablespoons (30 ml) water

2 tablespoons (30 ml) toasted sesame oil

2 tablespoons (30 ml) reduced-sodium tamari

½ cup (125 ml) unsalted natural peanut butter

1½ tablespoons (22 ml) minced fresh ginger

1½ tablespoons (22 ml) sliced green onion

1 tablespoon (15 ml) chopped fresh cilantro

1 teaspoon (5 ml) curry powder (see tip)

1 fresh hot chile, seeded (optional)

1 clove garlic, minced

¼ teaspoon (1 ml) freshly ground black pepper

Put all the ingredients in a blender in the order listed and process until smooth.

tip: For an extra-spicy version, use a hot Indian curry powder.

SERVING SUGGESTION: Try adding Smooth-Sailing Peanut Sauce to a stir-fry or use it as a dipping sauce.

MAKES 1½ CUPS (375 ML)

Per ¼ cup:

215 calories

6 g protein

1 g fat (19 g sat)

5 g carbohydrates

242 mg sodium

8 mg calcium

1 g fiber

Cashew and Macadamia Cheese Sauce

Rich and nutritious, blended nuts are the perfect stand-in for dairy ingredients. You'll never miss the moo.

½ cup (125 ml) raw cashews

½ cup (125 ml) raw macadamia nuts

½ cup (125 ml) water, plus more as needed

1½ teaspoons (7 ml) fresh rosemary leaves

1 clove garlic, minced

½ red bell pepper, coarsely chopped

½ teaspoon (2 ml) vegetable oil

¼ cup (60 ml) olive oil

Juice of ½ lemon

2 tablespoons (30 ml) nutritional yeast flakes

1 tablespoon (15 ml) thinly sliced fresh chives

1 teaspoon (5 ml) salt

¼ teaspoon (1 ml) ground white pepper

¼ teaspoon (1 ml) onion powder

MAKES 2½ CUPS (625 ML)

Per ¼ cup:
139 calories
2 g protein
14 g fat (1 g sat)
4 g carbohydrates
229 mg sodium
9 mg calcium
1 g fiber

Put the cashews, macadamia nuts, water, rosemary, and garlic in a large bowl and let soak until the nuts are soft, 2 to 4 hours.

Preheat the oven to 375 degrees F (190 degrees C).

Put the bell pepper in a small baking pan and drizzle with the vegetable oil. Bake for 15 minutes, until beginning to blacken. Let cool.

Put the nut mixture, bell pepper, olive oil, lemon juice, nutritional yeast, chives, salt, pepper, and onion powder in a blender and process until smooth and creamy. If the sauce seems too thick, add more water, 1 tablespoon (15 ml) at a time, until the desired consistency is achieved.

SERVING SUGGESTION: This cheesy sauce is a delightful topping for pizzas and tacos. It's also an excellent sandwich spread.

Passionate about Pesto

Pesto is a classic, and why not? The fresh herbs captivate with their aromas and crisp, clean taste. Make someone's day: make pesto.

> 2 cups (500 ml) basil leaves, packed and minced
>
> ½ cup (125 ml) flat-leaf parsley, packed and minced
>
> ½ cup (125 ml) pine nuts or macadamia nuts, toasted (see tip) and finely chopped
>
> ½ cup (125 ml) olive oil
>
> 1 tablespoon (15 ml) nutritional yeast flakes
>
> 2 cloves garlic, minced
>
> 1 teaspoon (5 ml) salt
>
> ¼ teaspoon (1 ml) ground white pepper

Put all the ingredients in a medium bowl and stir until well combined. Alternatively, for a faster but smoother pesto, put all the ingredients in a blender or food processor and process or pulse until well combined.

If you prefer the pesto warm, transfer it to a small saucepan and warm over low heat, stirring frequently, until heated through, about 5 minutes.

Stored in a sealed container in the freezer, the pesto will keep for 3 months.

tip: Put the pine nuts in a small skillet over medium heat and cook, stirring almost constantly, until lightly browned and fragrant, 2 to 3 minutes.

SERVING SUGGESTION: Use pesto as a pizza sauce or toss with hot pasta.

MAKES 2½ CUPS (625 ML)

Per ¼ cup:

145 calories

2 g protein

16 g fat (3 g sat)

2 g carbohydrates

230 mg sodium

13 mg calcium

1 g fiber

Delphinapterus leucas 600 F

RÉPUBLIQUE DE DJIBOUTI 2013

Punk Rock Gravy

Once you've tasted this gravy, you may never want another. It is seriously lovely, and it can be made in only fifteen minutes (which can be a fun time if the punk rock is blasting).

½ cup (125 ml) **olive oil**

1 small onion, finely diced

2 Thai chiles, seeded and minced (see tip)

3 fresh sage leaves, halved, or ½ teaspoon (2 ml) rubbed sage

1 teaspoon (5 ml) **freshly ground black pepper**

5 tablespoons (75 ml) **unbleached all-purpose flour**

4 cups (1 L) **water**

½ cup (125 ml) **nutritional yeast flakes**

½ cup (125 ml) **reduced-sodium tamari**

MAKES 5 CUPS (1.25 L)

Per ¼ cup:
149 calories
4 g protein
13 g fat (2 g sat)
4 g carbohydrates
320 mg sodium
19 mg calcium
1 g fiber

Heat the oil in a medium saucepan over high heat. When the oil is hot, add the onion, chiles, sage, and pepper. Cook, stirring frequently, until the onions begin to brown, about 5 minutes.

Add the flour and cook for 2 minutes, stirring constantly to prevent it from sticking to the pan and burning (this step prevents the gravy from having a floury taste).

Add the water, ½ cup (125 ml) at a time, whisking constantly to prevent lumps from forming. Whisk in the nutritional yeast and tamari. Cook, whisking frequently, until the desired consistency is achieved, about 8 minutes. Keep in mind that the gravy will thicken as it cools.

tip: If the gravy turns out lumpy, put it in a blender and process briefly. Just be sure to crack the lid to allow steam from the hot gravy to escape. The gravy will thicken as it cools. When reheating leftovers, add a small amount of water, 1 tablespoon (15 ml) at a time, until the desired consistency is achieved.

Variation: If you like heat, try adding 1 to 2 additional chiles.

Hummus Topped with Cilantro Salsa

Hummus is a classic staple for vegans around the globe, but this version is uniquely bejeweled with a savory salsa. With just minor adjustments, you can make one or more of the following variations, which feature their own intriguing flavors and colors.

HUMMUS

2 cups (500 ml) no-salt-added cooked or canned chickpeas, rinsed and drained

¼ cup (60 ml) tahini

2 tablespoons (30 ml) olive oil

2 tablespoons (30 ml) water

Zest of ½ lemon

Juice of 1 lemon

1 clove garlic, minced

½ teaspoon (2 ml) salt

¼ teaspoon (1 ml) freshly ground black pepper

SALSA

¼ cup (60 ml) coarsely chopped fresh cilantro

1 tomato, diced

Pinch salt

Pinch pepper

¼ lemon, cut into 3 wedges

Olive oil, for drizzling (optional)

To make the hummus, put all the ingredients in a food processor and process until smooth. Transfer to a small serving bowl.

To make the salsa, put the cilantro, tomato, salt, and pepper in a small bowl and stir until combined. Spoon the salsa on top of the hummus. Top the salsa with a squeeze of fresh lemon juice and a drizzle of olive oil if desired.

SERVING SUGGESTION: This is a great dish to serve at a party, alongside a big bowl of corn chips for dipping.

Red Pepper Hummus: Add 1 red bell pepper, coarsely chopped, to the food processor with the other ingredients when making the hummus.

Basil Salsa: Replace the cilantro in the salsa with an equal amount of fresh basil leaves.

Parsley Salsa: Replace the cilantro in the salsa with an equal amount of fresh parsley.

MAKES 2 CUPS (500 ML)
HUMMUS
AND 1 CUP (250 ML)
SALSA

Per ¼ cup hummus and
2 tablespoons salsa:

157 calories

5 g protein

10 g fat (1 g sat)

12 g carbohydrates

150 mg sodium

57 mg calcium

3 g fiber

Note: Analysis does not
include olive oil for drizzling.

Olive and Raisin Tapenade

Olives and raisins are an unexpected pairing that provides the perfect balance of salty and sweet. They perform without fault in this gloriously seasoned spread, which also features sun-dried tomatoes.

1 cup (250 ml) sun-dried tomatoes packed in oil, well drained

1 cup (250 ml) pitted kalamata olives

¼ cup (60 ml) raisins

1 tablespoon (15 ml) olive oil

1 clove garlic

MAKES 1¼ CUPS (310 ML)

Per ¼ cup:
361 calories
10 g protein
33 g fat (1 g sat)
35 g carbohydrates
197 mg sodium
10 mg calcium
0 g fiber

Put all the ingredients in a food processor and process into a thick paste. Continue processing until the mixture is as chunky or smooth as you like.

SERVING SUGGESTION: There are countless uses for this savory spread. For example, slather it over toasted bread or stir it into hot pasta or rice.

Laura Dakin,
CHIEF COOK, *STEVE IRWIN*

"Action stations!" The response I feel is quite immediate. I'm excited. What a joy it is to realize that the whaling fleet will almost certainly not have the opportunity to kill another whale. From experience, we know that after a few attempts to shake us off, they'll most likely turn for home, defeated.

During this time, the galley crew's main responsibility is to have a hot drink simmering on the stove and snacks at the ready. We also prepare a safe, warm environment for crew to return to after many hours out in the cold. And in the unlikely event of an emergency, it falls to us to provide the necessary medical environment.

The crew is full of energy and prepared to work nonstop. We'll do whatever we have to do, take any necessary action, for as long as we have to. We'll do anything to shut down the whaling operation and send the poachers home.

Cashew and Roasted Garlic Pâté

Slowly roasting garlic removes its sharpness, making it safe to use in large quantities. That's the secret to giving this pâté a pleasant garlic flavor but no sharp garlicky aftertaste.

1 bulb garlic, separated into cloves and peeled

¼ cup (60 ml) olive oil

1 cup (250 ml) raw cashews

1 cup (250 ml) no-salt-added cooked or canned white beans, rinsed and drained

¼ cup (60 ml) plain unsweetened nondairy milk

3 tablespoons (45 ml) nutritional yeast flakes

1 teaspoon (5 ml) salt

MAKES 2½ CUPS (625 ML)

Per ¼ cup:

147 calories

5 g protein

11 g fat (1 g sat)

9 g carbohydrates

233 mg sodium

15 mg calcium

2 g fiber

Preheat the oven to 300 degrees F (150 degrees C).

Put the garlic cloves in a small baking dish and cover with the oil. Bake for 20 minutes. Let cool.

Put the garlic and oil in a blender or food processor and process until smooth. Add the cashews, beans, milk, nutritional yeast, and salt and process until smooth.

SERVING SUGGESTION: Serve as you would any pâté—with crackers, on toast, or alongside crudités. Just make sure there's plenty to go around.

Can't Beet It Chutney

If you think beets are underappreciated, here's your chance to give them some love. Sweetened with raisins, this unusual chutney will draw oohs and aahs for its striking color and flavor.

12 small cooked and peeled beets, grated

1 onion, minced

¾ cup (185 ml) malt vinegar or cider vinegar

2 tablespoons (30 ml) raisins

2 tablespoons (30 ml) granulated sugar

1 tablespoon (15 ml) vegetable oil

1 clove garlic, crushed

Put all the ingredients in a large saucepan over medium heat. Cook, stirring occasionally, for 20 minutes. Remove from the heat and let cool. Gently mash before serving. Stored in a tightly sealed container in the refrigerator, Can't Beet It Chutney will keep for 3 weeks.

SERVING SUGGESTION: Give this chutney a try as a sandwich filling.

MAKES 2 CUPS (500 ML)

Per ¼ cup:

81 calories

2 g protein

2 g fat (1 g sat)

17 g carbohydrates

81 mg sodium

20 mg calcium

3 g fiber

Moo-Free Sour Cream

Calling all sour cream fans. Yes, there is a dairy-free version that tastes like the original. Here's the proof.

8 ounces (225 g) silken tofu

¼ cup (60 ml) plain unsweetened soy milk

Juice of 1 lemon

1 tablespoon (15 ml) vegetable oil

1 teaspoon (5 ml) ground white pepper

½ teaspoon (2 ml) salt

MAKES 2 CUPS (500 ML)

Put all the ingredients in a blender and process until smooth and creamy.

SERVING SUGGESTION: Serve over a baked potato or add to a veggie wrap.

Per ¼ cup:

36 calories

2 g protein

3 g fat (0.4 g sat)

1 g carbohydrates

151 mg sodium

16 mg calcium

0 g fiber

Creamy Dill Mayonnaise

It's important to use very cold soy milk for this mayo, so put some in the fridge for several hours before starting the recipe. While you'll be tempted to add this mayo to almost everything (yes, it tastes that good!), keep in mind that it's rich (just as mayo ought to be), so use it judiciously.

2 cups (500 ml) vegetable oil

1 cup (250 ml) full-fat plain unsweetened soy milk, chilled

1 tablespoon (15 ml) cider vinegar

2 teaspoons (10 ml) salt

2 teaspoons (10 ml) Dijon mustard

1 teaspoon (5 ml) dried dill weed

Put the oil and milk in a blender and process until thick and creamy. Add the vinegar and process or pulse for only a few seconds, just until incorporated. Transfer to a bowl and stir in the salt, mustard, and dill weed until well combined.

MAKES 3 CUPS (750 ML)

Per 2 tablespoons:
169 calories
0 g protein
19 g fat (6 g sat)
0 g carbohydrates
202 mg sodium
1 mg calcium
0 g fiber

Savory Tofu Feta

Here's one flavor-packed staple you'll always be glad to have in the fridge. The longer the tofu is marinated, the better it will taste.

1 cup (250 ml) olive oil

2 tablespoons (30 ml) nutritional yeast flakes

Juice of 2 lemons

6 cloves garlic, crushed

1 tablespoon (15 ml) dried oregano

2 teaspoons (10 ml) dried dill weed

2 teaspoons (10 ml) salt

1 teaspoon (5 ml) crushed red chile flakes

½ teaspoon (2 ml) freshly ground black pepper

2 pounds (900 grams) firm tofu, drained and cubed

MAKES 8 SERVINGS

Per serving:

220 calories

14 g protein

18 g fat (2 g sat)

2 g carbohydrates

292 mg sodium

138 mg calcium

0 g fiber

Put the oil, nutritional yeast, lemon juice, garlic, oregano, dill weed, salt, chile flakes, and pepper in a large bowl and stir until well combined. Add the tofu and gently stir until evenly coated.

Transfer the tofu and marinade to a storage container and seal tightly. Let marinate in the refrigerator for at least 1 hour before serving.

Stored in a sealed container in the refrigerator, Savory Tofu Feta will keep for 3 weeks. For the best results, occasionally stir the tofu and marinade to promote an even distribution of flavors.

SERVING SUGGESTION: You'll be tempted to snack on this as is, and it's also great as a salad topping or sandwich filler.

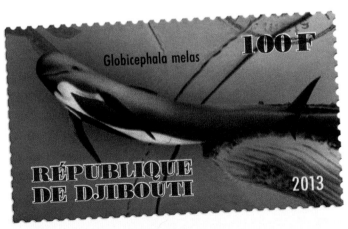

Compassionate Bacon Flakes

When you need your bacon fix, whip up this fine plant-based version. It's quite an amazing trick, combining flavor and compassion.

¼ cup (60 ml) **vegetable oil**

3 tablespoons (45 ml) **reduced-sodium tamari**

2 tablespoons (30 ml) **paprika**

1 tablespoon (15 ml) **nutritional yeast flakes**

1 tablespoon (15 ml) **liquid smoke**

2 teaspoons (10 ml) **beet powder** (optional; for enhanced color and nutrition)

1 teaspoon (5 ml) **salt**

5 cups (1.25 L) **unsweetened coconut flakes**

Preheat the oven to 300 degrees F (150 degrees C). Line two baking sheets with parchment paper.

Put the oil, tamari, paprika, nutritional yeast, liquid smoke, optional beet powder, and salt in a medium bowl and stir until well combined. Add the coconut flakes and stir until well coated.

Spread in a single layer on the lined baking sheets and bake for 15 minutes. Remove from the oven and let cool on the baking sheets (the bacon flakes will become crisp as they cool).

Stored in a sealed container, Compassionate Bacon Flakes will keep in the refrigerator for 2 months or at room temperature for 1 month.

SERVING SUGGESTION: Sprinkle on top of salads or add to tofu scrambles.

MAKES 10 SERVINGS

Per serving:

419 calories

5 g protein

38 g fat (30 g sat)

13 g carbohydrates

464 mg sodium

8 mg calcium

9 g fiber

BREADS

Making bread is an everyday job while we're on campaign—and we make a lot of it. The crew can easily finish off as many as eight loaves in twenty-four hours. Sometimes, if the weather permits and crew members are free to join us in the galley, I invite them for an impromptu bread-making workshop.

Although some people are intimidated by the thought of making bread at home, it's really not very hard. Of course, making bread aboard ship can be a slightly more challenging matter. A ship tossing on the Southern Ocean doesn't provide the ideal setting for baking anything, let alone bread! But with a few little adjustments to standard procedures, we make it work. For example, we use slightly warmer water to counter the freezing flour (our dry storage area is cold), we use a little more yeast, and we let the dough rise on top of the warm oven.

Tips for Making Perfect Bread

What food is more comforting than a hot loaf straight out of the oven? Following are my suggestions for successfully making bread:

- Mix the yeast with lukewarm water. If the water is too hot, it will kill the yeast; if it's too cold, it will not activate the yeast.

- Don't skimp on the kneading.

- Be patient and allow the dough to rise.

- If it looks like the dough isn't rising, roll it flat and cook it on the stove top, just like you would cook Nautical Naan (page 126). You can't go wrong!

Basic White Bread

This is my favorite basic bread recipe, and I use it as the foundation for many different kinds of breads. If you have this down, you can easily make white rolls and pizza dough, for example.

6 cups (1.5 L) unbleached all-purpose flour, plus more for kneading

2 tablespoons (30 ml) granulated sugar

1½ tablespoons (22 ml) active dry yeast

1 tablespoon (15 ml) salt

2½ cups (625 ml) warm water

2 tablespoons (30 ml) vegetable oil

MAKES 2 LOAVES, 12 SLICES PER LOAF

Per 2 slices:

256 calories

6 g protein

3 g fat (1 g sat)

50 g carbohydrates

571 mg sodium

5 mg calcium

2 g fiber

Note: Analysis does not include extra flour for kneading.

Put the flour, sugar, yeast, and salt in a large bowl. Put the water and oil in a large measuring cup and stir to combine. Pour the wet ingredients into the dry ingredients and stir with a wooden spoon until a dough forms.

Turn the dough out onto a well-floured surface and knead until smooth and elastic, about 20 minutes. Add more flour as necessary to prevent the dough from becoming too sticky.

Lightly oil a large bowl (preferably wooden). Transfer the dough to the bowl, cover with a clean, damp tea towel, and set in a warm place out of direct sunlight to rise until doubled in size, about 1 hour.

Punch down the dough and transfer it to a lightly floured surface, shape it into a ball, and cut it in half with a sharp knife. Form each half into a loaf shape and transfer to two 9 x 5 x 3-inch (23 x 13 x 8 cm) loaf pans. Gently press the dough into the pans (the dough should fill each pan about halfway). Cover with a clean, damp tea towel and set in a warm place out of direct sunlight, until the dough has doubled in size, about 1 hour.

Preheat the oven to 350 degrees F (180 degrees C).

Bake for 35 to 40 minutes, until golden brown. Let cool in the pans for 30 minutes. Transfer to a cooling rack and let cool completely before wrapping in plastic.

tip: After the first rising, shape the dough if desired. For example, braid it on a well-floured surface before putting it in the bread pans for the second rising. If making pizza, this is the time to roll out the dough on a well-floured surface to form shells.

Onion and Herb Dinner Rolls

A basket of steaming rolls on the table is a wonderful and welcome sight. Eager diners can smear them with vegan butter and nibble on them as the meal is being served or use them to mop up tasty sauces or broths as they eat.

2½ cups (625 ml) unbleached all-purpose flour, plus more for kneading

¼ red onion, thinly sliced

2 tablespoons (30 ml) minced fresh basil

2 teaspoons (10 ml) active dry yeast

1 teaspoon (5 ml) granulated sugar

1 teaspoon (5 ml) salt

1½ cups (375 ml) warm water

1½ teaspoons (7 ml) vegetable oil

Put the flour, onion, basil, yeast, sugar, and salt in a large bowl. Put the water and oil in a large measuring cup and stir to combine. Pour the wet ingredients into the dry ingredients. Stir with a wooden spoon until a dough forms.

Turn the dough out onto a well-floured surface and knead until smooth and elastic, about 20 minutes. Add more flour as necessary to prevent the dough from becoming too sticky.

Lightly oil a large bowl (preferably wooden). Transfer the dough to the bowl, cover with a clean, damp tea towel, and set in a warm place out of direct sunlight to rise until doubled in size, about 1 hour.

Dust a shallow rimmed baking sheet with flour.

Punch down the dough and turn it out onto a well-floured surface. Divide the dough into eight equal portions and roll each portion into a ball. Arrange on the floured baking sheet, making sure there is plenty of room in between the balls. Cover with a clean, damp tea towel and let rise until the dough has doubled in size, about 1 hour.

Preheat the oven to 350 degrees F (180 degrees C).

Bake for 20 to 25 minutes, until golden brown. Transfer to a cooling rack and let cool for 5 minutes before serving.

MAKES 8 ROLLS

Per roll:

154 calories

4 g protein

1 g fat (0.4 g sat)

30 g carbohydrates

286 mg sodium

3 mg calcium

1 g fiber

Note: Analysis does not include extra flour for kneading.

Overboard for Aloo Paratha

This potato-filled bread can be made anytime, but we especially like to serve it for breakfast on a cold day.

DOUGH

2 cups (500 ml) unbleached all-purpose flour, plus more for kneading and rolling

Pinch salt

½ cup (125 ml) minced green onions

½ cup (125 ml) water

FILLING

4 cups (1 L) water

3 potatoes, scrubbed (peeling optional) and cubed (about 3½ cups/875 ml)

Pinch salt

2 tablespoons (30 ml) coconut oil, plus more for cooking the paratha

3 cloves garlic, minced

20 fresh curry leaves

2 Thai chiles, seeded and minced

1 tablespoon (15 ml) minced fresh ginger

1 tablespoon (15 ml) black mustard seeds

1 tablespoon (15 ml) black cumin seeds

**MAKES 8 PARATHAS,
4 SERVINGS**

Per serving:

370 calories

9 g protein

7 g fat (0.4 g sat)

65 g carbohydrates

3 mg sodium

11 mg calcium

4 g fiber

Note: Analysis does not include extra flour for kneading.

To make the dough, sift the flour and salt into a large bowl. Add the green onions and water and stir with a wooden spoon until a dough forms. Gently knead the dough until it is tacky and elastic. If the dough is very sticky, add a small amount of additional flour as you knead. Transfer to a large bowl and cover with a clean, damp tea towel while you prepare the filling.

To make the filling, put the water, potatoes, and salt in a medium saucepan over high heat and bring to a boil. Decrease the heat to medium-high and cook until fork-tender, 15 to 20 minutes. Remove from the heat, drain, and mash.

Heat the oil in a large skillet over medium heat. When the oil is hot, add the garlic, curry leaves, chiles, ginger, mustard seeds, and cumin and cook, stirring frequently so the spices don't burn, for 5 minutes. Add the potato and stir until well combined. Remove from the heat and let cool.

As soon as the filling is cool enough to handle, begin to stuff the dough. Transfer the dough to a lightly floured surface and divide it into eight equal portions. Lightly oil a large plate. Roll each portion of dough into a ball. Flatten a ball between your hands to form a disk and put on the prepared plate. Put 1 tablespoon (15 ml) of filling in the center of the disk. Gather up the ends and bring them together at the top (like a drawstring purse). Press the edges together to create a secure seal. Press into a disk with your hands; the dough should enclose the filling.

Transfer to a lightly floured surface. Gently flatten the disk with a rolling pin (it's okay if a little bit of potato finds its way out).

Sprinkle a large plate with flour. Put the stuffed dough on the plate. Repeat with the remaining dough and filling.

Line a large plate with paper towels. Oil a large skillet with coconut oil and heat over high heat. When the oil is hot, carefully put one piece of stuffed dough in the skillet; the oil may splatter, so take care that you don't get burned. Cook until the bottom becomes browned in spots, 30 to 40 seconds. Flip over and cook the other side until browned in spots, 30 to 40 seconds. Transfer the cooked bread to the lined plate to remove any excess oil. Repeat with the remaining dough, adding more oil to the skillet and adjusting the heat as needed.

SERVING SUGGESTION: Paratha is best served hot with a spicy fruit chutney as an accompaniment.

TKI·844

GOVERNMENT OF JAPAN

Chad Halstead,
BOSUN AND SMALL-BOAT DRIVER, *STEVE IRWIN*

Word rushes through the 200-foot-long ship like wildfire. Crew members from all departments race from stem to stern, repeating the same message: The whaling fleet is straight off our bow. Captain's orders are "stand by for action."

We've been waiting days, weeks, months for this moment. The deck crew has been training and preparing for this confrontation. Quickly, we drop what we are doing and rush out on deck to ready the ship. Crew members execute the designated tasks we've been rehearsing for weeks now. Deckhands uncover the small boats and warm up the engines, while the bosun's mate readies the crane that's used to drop the boats into the water.

I'm part of the small-boat crew and, after putting on special dry suits and helmets, we go straight to the bridge to get the mission briefing from the captain. The boat navigators copy down all coordinates—targets, distance, and GPS. Then we head back down onto the boat deck to begin the launch.

Within minutes of the initial alarm, the mechanical orchestration begins. The crane lifts the small boats from their cradles, swings them high across the deck, and drops them into the water. The crews climb down the ladder to board the small boats. The engines growl into gear. Seconds later, we speed ahead to intercept our targets. Heartbeats race, adrenaline rises, nerves come to life.

From my vantage point, so low on the water, the objects on the horizon grow from small gray dots into the outline of ships. I first identify the massive silhouette of the factory whaling vessel, the *Nisshin Maru*. Shortly after that, I spot the killing ships, with their unmistakable harpoon decks lifted.

Racing closer and closer, we ride a roller coaster of waves, quickly closing the gap. For once we outspeed and outmaneuver even the fastest of whaling ships. As we approach, I see the crews running frantically on the decks of the harpoon ships, pulling protective nets and anti-boarding spikes along the sides. They start up their water cannons in hopes of fending us off. I begin to count down the seconds until intercept.

For a moment, time stands still. I pull alongside, just meters away from the hull of a whaling ship. I almost reach out and touch it, as if to ensure it's actually real. I have seen images of these infamous vessels, but now this one is right here. *And so am I.*

I look around for a second, realizing that in a world of seven billion people, my crewmates and I are the only ones here to fight this battle. And I see not just a ship, but a 130-meter-long, 8,000-ton machine designed for one purpose: killing an innocent and highly intelligent marine species. And that's exactly what it's here to do—in an area designated as a whale sanctuary.

The sound of the ship's alarm and the heavy bounce of the waves pulls me out of my thoughts. I'm part of a small group that is dedicated to standing in this ship's way. Our mission is simple and clear: shut down this illegal Japanese whaling fleet.

GOLIATH

Nautical Naan

Naan is not only the ultimate invention for transporting curry from your plate to your mouth, but it can also be paired with an endless variety of fillings to become a satisfying veggie wrap.

6 cups (1.5 L) unbleached all-purpose flour, plus more for kneading and rolling

2 tablespoons (30 ml) granulated sugar

1½ tablespoons (22 ml) active dry yeast

1 teaspoon (5 ml) salt

2½ cups (625 ml) warm water

2 tablespoons (30 ml) vegetable oil

MAKES 8 LARGE NAAN

Per naan:
385 calories
10 g protein
4 g fat (1 g sat)
74 g carbohydrates
3 mg sodium
8 mg calcium
3 g fiber

Note: Analysis does not include extra flour for kneading.

Put the flour, sugar, yeast, and salt in a large bowl. Put the water and oil in a large measuring cup and stir to combine. Pour the wet ingredients into the dry ingredients. Stir with a wooden spoon until a dough forms.

Turn the dough out onto a well-floured surface and knead until smooth and elastic, about 20 minutes. Add more flour as necessary to prevent the dough from becoming too sticky.

Lightly oil a large bowl (preferably wooden). Transfer the dough to the bowl, cover with a clean, damp tea towel, and set in a warm place out of direct sunlight to rise until doubled in size, about 1 hour. Punch down the dough and turn it out onto a well-floured surface.

Lightly oil a large plate. Divide the dough into eight equal portions, roll each portion into a ball, and put the balls on the plate.

Dust a large plate with flour. Transfer one ball to a well-floured surface and roll it into a thin oval or circle. Transfer to the plate. Repeat with the remaining dough.

Line a large plate with paper towels. Generously oil a large skillet with coconut oil and heat over high heat. When the oil is hot, carefully put one piece of rolled dough in the skillet; the oil may splatter, so take care that you don't get burned. Cook until the bottom becomes browned in spots, 30 to 40 seconds. Flip over and cook the other side until browned in spots, 30 to 40 seconds. Transfer to the lined plate to remove any excess oil. Repeat with the remaining rolled dough, adding more oil to the skillet and adjusting the heat as needed.

Swedish Flatbread

Traditional crispbread, native to Scandinavian countries, is a thin, unleavened, wafer-like bread. It's a healthy, low-calorie, whole-grain snack that pairs well with just about anything, from hot soups to creamy spreads.

 2 cups (500 ml) unbleached all-purpose flour

 1 cup (250 ml) rye flour

 ½ cup (125 ml) raw sesame seeds

 1½ teaspoons (7 ml) salt

 1¼ cups (310 ml) warm water

 ¼ cup (60 ml) vegetable oil

MAKES 10 SERVINGS

Per serving:

218 calories

5 g protein

9 g fat (2 g sat)

29 g carbohydrates

344 mg sodium

7 mg calcium

3 g fiber

Put the all-purpose flour, rye flour, sesame seeds, and salt in a large bowl and stir until well combined. Put the water and oil in a large measuring cup and stir to combine. Slowly pour the liquid into the dry mixture and stir constantly with a wooden spoon until a dough forms. Turn out the dough onto a lightly floured surface and knead until smooth and elastic. Add flour as necessary to prevent the dough from becoming too sticky. Cover with a clean, damp tea towel and let stand while the oven heats up.

Preheat the oven to 400 degrees F (205 degrees C).

Turn the dough out onto a well-floured surface and divide it into six equal pieces. Roll out one piece of dough as thin as possible and carefully transfer it to a shallow rimmed baking sheet. The dough can be any shape as long as it fits flat on the baking sheet. Bake for 5 minutes and remove from the oven. Flip the flatbread over and bake for 1 minute longer, just until it begins to brown. Let cool on a rack. The flatbread will become crispier as it cools. Repeat with the remaining dough.

SERVING SUGGESTION: Break the flatbread into different sizes and shapes before serving or storing. Serve alongside a bowl of hummus for dipping. Try Hummus Topped with Cilantro Salsa (page 107).

Big Boat Banana Bread

A wonderful way to eat banana bread is warm, smeared with vegan butter. After it cools, banana bread will keep in the fridge for several days. This loaf will give you leftovers to keep on hand for a quick-fix breakfast or afternoon snack.

BATTER

5 very ripe bananas, mashed

¾ cup (185 ml) light brown sugar

½ cup (125 ml) applesauce

½ cup (125 ml) vegetable oil

½ cup (125 ml) vegan butter

¼ cup (60 ml) plain or vanilla nondairy milk

1 tablespoon (15 ml) ground cinnamon

1 tablespoon (15 ml) psyllium husks

1 tablespoon (15 ml) vanilla extract

Pinch salt

3 cups (750 ml) unbleached all-purpose flour

2 teaspoons (10 ml) baking powder

½ teaspoon (2 ml) baking soda

TOPPING

2 tablespoons (30 ml) ground almonds

2 tablespoons (30 ml) old-fashioned rolled oats

2 tablespoons (30 ml) light brown sugar

Preheat the oven to 350 degrees F (180 degrees C). Line a 9 x 5-inch (23 x 13 cm) loaf pan with parchment paper and set aside.

To make the batter, put the bananas, sugar, applesauce, oil, butter, milk, cinnamon, psyllium husks, vanilla extract, and salt in a large bowl. Stir until well combined.

Sift the flour, baking powder, and baking soda into the bowl. Stir until well incorporated.

To make the topping, put all the ingredients in a small bowl. Stir until well combined.

Scrape the batter into the lined pan using a rubber spatula. Sprinkle the topping evenly over the batter. Bake for 25 to 30 minutes, until a toothpick inserted in the center of the loaf comes out clean. Let cool in the pan for 10 minutes before removing and transferring to a rack. Cool completely before slicing.

MAKES 16 SLICES

Per slice:

290 calories

3 g protein

13 g fat (4 g sat)

40 g carbohydrates

132 mg sodium

40 mg calcium

2 g fiber

Captain's Favorite Carrot Cake,
page 138

SWEETS AND TREATS

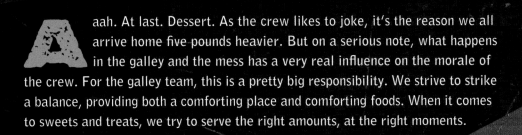

Aaah. At last. Dessert. As the crew likes to joke, it's the reason we all arrive home five pounds heavier. But on a serious note, what happens in the galley and the mess has a very real influence on the morale of the crew. For the galley team, this is a pretty big responsibility. We strive to strike a balance, providing both a comforting place and comforting foods. When it comes to sweets and treats, we try to serve the right amounts, at the right moments.

Aussie Anzac Cookies

Australian Anzac cookies are chewy and delicious. You may want to take my advice on this: freeze half of them as soon as they cool so you can't gobble down the whole batch all at once.

1 cup (250 ml) unbleached all-purpose flour

1 cup (250 ml) old-fashioned rolled oats

1 cup (250 ml) granulated sugar

¾ cup (185 ml) unsweetened shredded dried coconut

1 teaspoon (5 ml) salt

½ cup (125 ml) vegan butter

2 tablespoons (30 ml) maple syrup or agave nectar

1 tablespoon (15 ml) molasses

1 teaspoon (5 ml) vanilla extract

1 tablespoon (15 ml) boiling water

½ teaspoon (2 ml) baking soda

MAKES 20 COOKIES

Per cookie:
102 calories
2 g protein
6 g fat (3 g sat)
11 g carbohydrates
182 mg sodium
7 mg calcium
1 g fiber

Preheat the oven to 350 degrees F (180 degrees C). Line two baking sheets with parchment paper.

Put the flour, oats, sugar, coconut, and salt in a large bowl and stir to combine.

Heat the butter in a small saucepan over low heat until melted. Add the maple syrup, molasses, and vanilla extract and stir to combine. Remove from the heat.

Put the water and baking soda in a coffee mug and stir until combined. Immediately add to the butter mixture and stir until combined.

Pour the wet ingredients into the dry ingredients and stir until well combined to form a dough.

For each cookie, scoop out 1 rounded tablespoon (15 ml) of dough and drop it onto a lined baking sheet. Repeat with the remaining dough, leaving space between cookies for spreading.

Bake for 8 minutes. Let cool completely before serving or storing. Stored in a tightly sealed container at room temperature, Aussie Anzac Cookies will keep for about 5 days.

Peanut Butter Campaign Cookies

This classic treat, which has been tried and tested at least one million times in our fleet's galleys, will literally melt in your mouth. Cookies and commitment are the secrets to good morale.

2 cups (500 ml) unsalted natural peanut butter

1 cup (250 ml) granulated sugar

½ cup (125 ml) soft vegan butter

½ cup (125 ml) plain or vanilla soy milk or other nondairy milk

2 teaspoons (10 ml) vanilla extract

2 cups (500 ml) unbleached all-purpose flour

1 teaspoon (5 ml) baking soda

30 raw peanuts or pieces of vegan dark chocolate, for garnish

Preheat the oven to 350 degrees F (180 degrees C). Line a baking sheet with parchment paper.

Put the peanut butter, sugar, and butter in a large bowl and cream together with an electric mixer. Add the milk and vanilla extract and mix well. Sift the flour and baking soda into the bowl and mix until well combined to form a dough.

For each cookie, scoop 1 rounded tablespoon (15 ml) of dough into the palm of your hand, roll it into a ball, press it down slightly, and put it on the lined baking sheet. Repeat with the remaining dough, leaving 2 inches (5 cm) between cookies to allow for spreading. Press a single peanut into the center of each cookie for garnish.

Bake for 8 minutes. Let cool completely on the baking sheet before serving or storing (if you remove the cookies while they're still warm, they may fall apart). Stored in a tightly sealed container at room temperature, Peanut Butter Campaign Cookies will keep for about 5 days.

MAKES 30 COOKIES

Per cookie:

172 calories

5 g protein

12 g fat (3 g sat)

10 g carbohydrates

71 mg sodium

6 mg calcium

1 g fiber

Note: Analysis does not include raw peanuts or dark chocolate for garnish.

CANADA
46
BALAENA MYSTICETUS

Vera's Hungarian Chocolate Bread

Vera spends her annual vacation with us in the galley, working crazy hard and delighting us all with her amazing Hungarian dishes. This sweet bread is just one of many delicious dessert recipes she has mastered over the years.

DOUGH

1½ tablespoons (22 ml) orange marmalade

1½ tablespoons (22 ml) granulated sugar

1½ tablespoons (22 ml) vegan butter

3 cups (750 ml) unbleached all-purpose flour

¾ teaspoon (4 ml) salt

2 teaspoons (10 ml) active dry yeast

1 cup (250 ml) warm water

FILLING

½ cup (125 ml) vegan butter

¾ cup (185 ml) granulated sugar

¾ cup (185 ml) unsweetened cocoa powder, plus more for dusting the bread

Powdered sugar, for dusting the bread (optional)

MAKES 1 LARGE LOAF (OR TWO SMALLER LOAVES), 12 SERVINGS

Per serving:
221 calories
4 g protein
9 g fat (2 g sat)
29 g carbohydrates
221 mg sodium
10 mg calcium
3 g fiber

To make the dough, put the marmalade, sugar, and butter in a large bowl and beat with a whisk until well combined.

Sift the flour and salt into a large bowl. Add the yeast and stir until well combined. Add the flour mixture to the butter mixture, then slowly add the water, stirring constantly, until a dough forms.

Turn the dough out onto a well-floured surface and knead until smooth and elastic, about 15 minutes. Add more flour as necessary to prevent the dough from becoming too sticky. Cover with a clean, damp tea towel and set in a warm place out of direct sunlight to rise until doubled in size, about 50 minutes.

While the dough is rising, make the filling. Put all the ingredients in a food processor and process until smooth. Refrigerate until the dough has risen.

Punch down the dough and turn it out onto a well-floured surface. Roll out with a rolling pin, forming a rectangle about ¼-inch (½ cm) thick. Spread the filling evenly over the dough using a rubber spatula.

Preheat the oven to 350 degrees F (180 degrees C). Lightly flour a baking sheet.

Roll the dough into a long log, making sure you roll it fairly tightly, and put it on the floured baking sheet (if you prefer, you can make two smaller logs). Set in a warm place out of direct sunlight until doubled in size, about 30 minutes.

Bake for 25 to 30 minutes. Let cool and dust with cocoa powder or powdered sugar or both before serving.

Action Coffee Cake

Baking a cake can be a major challenge when you're on a moving ship! One of the features that makes this cake good for seafarers is the fact that the batter is quite stiff, which means it doesn't slop around in the pan. Plus, the cake is wonderfully moist and delicious.

3 cups (750 ml) unbleached all-purpose flour

$\frac{1}{2}$ cup (125 ml) whole wheat flour

$\frac{1}{2}$ teaspoon (2 ml) baking powder

$\frac{1}{2}$ teaspoon (2 ml) baking soda

$\frac{1}{2}$ teaspoon (2 ml) salt

$1\frac{1}{2}$ cups (375 ml) granulated sugar

1 cup (250 ml) peeled and finely diced apple or pear

1 cup (250 ml) vegetable oil

$\frac{3}{4}$ cup (185 ml) plain or vanilla soy milk or other nondairy milk

$\frac{1}{2}$ cup (125 ml) applesauce

$\frac{1}{4}$ cup (60 ml) light brown sugar

$\frac{1}{4}$ cup (60 ml) ground almonds

Preheat the oven to 350 degrees F (180 degrees C). Line a 13 x 9-inch (33 x 23 cm) cake pan with parchment paper.

Sift the unbleached all-purpose flour, whole wheat flour, baking powder, baking soda, and salt into a large bowl. Add the sugar and apple and stir to combine.

Put the oil, milk, and applesauce in a large bowl and stir to combine.

Gently fold the wet ingredients into the dry ingredients using a rubber spatula until well combined. Scrape the batter into the lined cake pan using the rubber spatula. Sprinkle the brown sugar and almonds evenly over the top of the batter. Bake for 40 minutes, or until a toothpick inserted in the center of the cake comes out clean. Let cool before serving.

MAKES 16 SERVINGS

Per serving:

263 calories

4 g protein

16 g fat (4 g sat)

28 g carbohydrates

128 mg sodium

3 mg calcium

2 g fiber

Lemon-Poppy Seed Cake

We love citrus, which is loaded with vitamin C, and we love cake, so this combo is a natural and nutritious choice. Although poppy seeds are traditionally used in this recipe, chia seeds, which are also small and black, have become increasingly available. A good source of omega-3 fatty acids, tiny chia seeds are often categorized as a superfood.

BATTER

3 cups (750 ml) unbleached all-purpose flour

4 teaspoons (20 ml) baking powder

1/2 teaspoon (2 ml) baking soda

1 1/2 cups (375 ml) granulated sugar

1/2 cup (125 ml) poppy seeds, or 1/4 cup (60 ml) chia seeds

1/2 teaspoon (2 ml) salt

2 cups (500 ml) plain unsweetened coconut yogurt or vegan buttermilk (see tip)

1/2 cup (125 ml) vegan butter, melted

Zest of 2 lemons

Juice of 2 lemons

FROSTING

1/2 cup (125 ml) vegan butter

2 cups (500 ml) powdered sugar

Zest of 1/2 lemon

1/3 cup (85 ml) lemon juice

MAKES 8 SERVINGS

Per serving:
708 calories
7 g protein
28 g fat (11 g sat)
110 g carbohydrates
612 mg sodium
31 mg calcium
4 g fiber

Preheat the oven to 350 degrees F (180 degrees C). Line a 9-inch (23 cm) round cake pan with parchment paper.

To make the batter, sift the flour, baking powder, and baking soda into a large bowl and stir to combine. Add the sugar, poppy seeds, and salt and stir until well combined.

Put the yogurt, butter, zest, and juice in a small bowl and stir until well combined.

Add the wet ingredients to the dry ingredients and stir with a whisk until well combined. Scrape the batter into the prepared pan using a rubber spatula. Bake for 45 minutes, or until a toothpick inserted in the center comes out clean. Let cool in the pan.

To make the frosting, put all the ingredients in a food processor and process until smooth. Transfer to a small bowl and store in the refrigerator until the cake has cooled.

When the cake is completely cool, remove it from the pan and transfer to a serving dish. To frost the cake, spread the frosting over the top using a metal spatula.

tip: To make vegan buttermilk, put 2 cups (500 ml) of plain unsweetened soy milk in a small bowl. Add 1 tablespoon (15 ml) of white vinegar and stir until well combined.

Lime Explosion Cake

Created by Ronnie at the Anarchist Teapot in the United Kingdom, this citrusy confection is an absolute crew favorite. The name represents truth in advertising: each bite is like a lime explosion in your mouth!

BATTER
2½ cups (625 ml) self-rising flour (see tip)

2 teaspoons (10 ml) baking powder

1½ cups (375 ml) granulated sugar

Zest of 2 limes

1 cup (250 ml) vegan butter

Egg replacer to equal 4 eggs (see tip)

½ cup (125 ml) plain or vanilla soy milk or other nondairy milk

GLAZE
¾ cup (185 ml) powdered sugar

Juice of 3 limes

Preheat the oven to 350 degrees F (180 degrees C). Oil a 9-inch (23 cm) round cake pan.

To make the batter, sift the flour and baking powder into a large bowl. Add the sugar and zest and stir until well combined.

Heat the butter in a small saucepan over low heat until just melted. Add the egg replacer and milk and stir until combined.

Pour the wet ingredients into the dry ingredients and stir until well combined. Scrape the batter into the prepared pan using a rubber spatula. Bake for 40 minutes, or until a toothpick inserted in the center of the cake comes out clean. Let cool in the pan for 10 minutes.

To make the glaze, put the powdered sugar and juice in a small bowl and whisk until well combined. Spoon the glaze evenly over the cake. Serve the cake cool or still warm by spooning out portions onto plates.

tip: To make your own self-rising flour for this recipe, sift 2½ cups (625 ml) unbleached all-purpose flour, 2 tablespoons (30 ml) baking powder, and ½ teaspoon (2 ml) salt into a large bowl. Omit the 2 teaspoons (10 ml) baking powder in the recipe.

One commercially available egg substitute is called Ener-G Egg Replacer. To replace 4 eggs, use 2 tablespoons (30 ml) of Ener-G Egg Replacer dissolved in ½ cup (125 ml) of water.

Lemon Explosion Cake: Replace the lime zest in the cake with an equal amount of lemon zest and the lime juice in the glaze with an equal amount of lemon juice.

MAKES 8 SERVINGS

Per serving:

402 calories

4 g protein

22 g fat (6 g sat)

45 g carbohydrates

765 mg sodium

92 mg calcium

1 g fiber

Captain's Favorite Carrot Cake

No Sea Shepherd cookbook would be complete without Captain Paul's favorite dessert. This is one sweet way to eat your veggies.

CAKE

2 cups (500 ml) peeled and shredded carrots

1 cup (250 ml) dark brown sugar

1 cup (250 ml) vegetable oil

¾ cup (185 ml) apple juice

2 tablespoons (30 ml) ground flaxseeds

1 teaspoon (5 ml) vanilla extract

2½ cups (625 ml) unbleached all-purpose flour

1½ teaspoons (7 ml) baking powder

1 teaspoon (5 ml) baking soda

1 cup (250 ml) walnut pieces

1 teaspoon (5 ml) ground cinnamon

½ teaspoon (2 ml) ground nutmeg

½ teaspoon (2 ml) salt

¼ teaspoon (1 ml) ground cloves

FROSTING

8 ounces (225 grams) vegan cream cheese

1 tablespoon (15 ml) powdered sugar

Zest of ½ lemon

MAKES 8 SERVINGS

Per serving:
669 calories
8 g protein
46 g fat (12 g sat)
59 g carbohydrates
412 mg sodium
79 mg calcium
5 g fiber

Preheat the oven to 350 degrees F (180 degrees C). Line a 9-inch (23 cm) round cake pan with parchment paper.

To make the cake, put the carrots, brown sugar, oil, apple juice, flaxseeds, and vanilla extract in a large bowl and stir until well combined.

Sift the flour, baking powder, and baking soda into a large bowl. Add the walnuts, cinnamon, nutmeg, salt, and cloves and stir until combined.

Add the wet ingredients to the dry ingredients and stir until well combined. Scrape the batter into the lined pan using a rubber spatula. Bake for 25 to 30 minutes, or until a toothpick inserted in the center comes out clean. Let cool completely before removing from the pan.

To make the frosting, put all the ingredients in a food processor and process until smooth. Scrape the frosting into a small bowl, cover with plastic wrap, and refrigerate.

When the cake is completely cool, remove it from the pan and transfer to a serving dish. To frost the cake, spread the frosting over the top using a metal spatula.

Raw Cheesecake to the Rescue

Cheesecake, decadence is thy name! This raw version is delightfully rich as well as citrusy, thanks to the plentiful addition of lemon juice. I typically serve this dessert topped with blueberries, but any type of berry will do.

CRUST

2 cups (500 ml) raw macadamia nuts

1 cup (250 ml) pitted dates

1 tablespoon (15 ml) coconut oil

FILLING

3 cups (750 ml) raw cashew pieces, soaked in water for 2 to 4 hours and drained

1 cup (250 ml) freshly squeezed lemon juice

1 cup (250 ml) agave nectar

1 tablespoon (15 ml) coconut oil

1 teaspoon (5 ml) vanilla extract

½ teaspoon (2 ml) salt

TOPPING

1 cup (250 ml) fresh or thawed frozen blueberries, raspberries, or strawberries

To make the crust, put the macadamia nuts, dates, and coconut oil in a food processor and process until finely ground. Press the nut mixture firmly into the bottom and along the sides of a 9-inch (23 cm) springform pan. (If you find this difficult, put the pan containing the nut mixture into the freezer for 20 minutes. The mixture will become more firm and will be easier to press into the pan.)

To make the filling, put all the ingredients in a blender and process until smooth and creamy. Pour the filling into the crust.

Put the cheesecake in the freezer until firm, 3 to 4 hours. Before serving, transfer to the refrigerator and let thaw for 10 to 15 minutes. Carefully remove from the pan. Top with the blueberries or put them in a bowl and pass them at the table. Serve immediately.

MAKES 16 SERVINGS

Per serving:

356 calories

6 g protein

24 g fat (2 g sat)

36 g carbohydrates

75 mg sodium

34 mg calcium

3 g fiber

Chocolate-Banana Fudge Cake

Another crew favorite from the Anarchist Teapot in the United Kingdom, this rich, soft, and moist chocolate cake always goes fast. It's never around long enough for us to know how well it keeps!

BATTER

2½ cups (625 ml) unbleached all-purpose flour, plus more for sprinkling the pan

¾ cup (185 ml) unsweetened cocoa powder

2 tablespoons (30 ml) baking powder

2½ very ripe bananas

2½ cups (625 ml) brewed coffee, chilled

2 cups (500 ml) granulated sugar

2 cups (500 ml) vegetable oil

1 teaspoon (5 ml) vanilla extract

1 teaspoon (5 ml) salt

FUDGE SAUCE

½ cup (125 ml) vegan butter

¾ cup (185 ml) unsweetened cocoa powder

1 cup (250 ml) powdered sugar

¼ cup (60 ml) water

2 tablespoons (30 ml) rum (optional)

2 teaspoons (10 ml) vanilla extract

MAKES 16 SERVINGS

Per serving:

313 calories

4 g protein

21 g fat (6 g sat)

32 g carbohydrates

159 mg sodium

74 mg calcium

4 g fiber

Preheat the oven to 350 degrees F (180 degrees C). Generously mist a standard Bundt pan with nonstick cooking spray.

To make the batter, sift the flour, cocoa powder, and baking powder into a large bowl and stir until well combined.

Put the bananas, coffee, sugar, oil, vanilla extract, and salt in a large bowl. Mix until well combined using an electric mixer or immersion blender.

Pour the wet ingredients into the dry ingredients and stir until well combined. The batter will be fairly thin and runny.

Pour the batter into the prepared pan and bake for 50 minutes, or until a toothpick inserted in the center of the cake comes out clean. Let cool in the pan for 10 minutes, then invert the cake directly onto a serving dish.

To make the fudge sauce, heat the butter in a medium saucepan over medium-low heat until just melted. Add the cocoa powder and stir with a whisk until well combined. Add the powdered sugar, water, optional rum, and vanilla extract and stir almost constantly until the sauce just begins to bubble. Decrease the heat to low and cook, stirring frequently, until the sauce begins to thicken, about 15 minutes. Remove from the stove and let cool; the sauce will thicken as it cools.

When the cake has cooled and the sauce is about room temperature, pour the sauce over the cake and serve immediately.

tip: Be sure that the Bundt pan is generously misted with nonstick cooking spray before the batter is poured in so the cake will come out cleanly after baking.

Antarctic Tropical Canadian Delight

Captain Paul invented this unique concoction after a chunk of the Ross Ice Shelf, the world's largest body of floating ice, fell onto the *Steve Irwin's* deck. Although it's very simple, it's one of the best-tasting desserts I've ever had. So line up your shot glasses. And work quickly so the ice doesn't melt before you serve it.

6 cups (1.5 L) **shaved ice** (see tip)
½ cup (125 ml) **coconut-flavored rum**
8 teaspoons (40 ml) **Canadian maple syrup**

Put 1½ cups (375 ml) of ice in each of four ice-cream bowls. Put 2 tablespoons (30 ml) of rum in each of four shot glasses. Put 2 teaspoons (10 ml) of maple syrup in each of four shot glasses.

Serve each bowl alongside a shot glass with the rum and a shot glass with the maple syrup. Instruct each member of your dessert crew to add the rum and maple syrup to the ice just before digging in.

tip: Shaved ice is preferable, but well-crushed ice will also work. And, by all means, use glacier ice if you can get it.

MAKES 4 SERVINGS

Per serving:
131 calories
0 g protein
0 g fat (0 g sat)
22 g carbohydrates
10 mg sodium
2 mg calcium
0 g fiber

Australia 35c
SOUTHERN RIGHT WHALE

Hot Chile Chocolate

Our tradition is to serve Hot Chile Chocolate to the crew returning from action. And this "hot" hot cocoa will warm you up on a cold and blustery day, just like it does the crew aboard ship.

⅓ cup (85 ml) plain or vanilla nondairy milk

4 tablespoons (60 ml) unsweetened cocoa powder

4 cups (1L) water

3 tablespoons (45 ml) granulated sugar

1 hot chile, halved and seeded

½ cup (125 ml) nondairy creamer or milk

Pinch ground cinnamon (optional)

½ teaspoon (2 ml) vanilla extract (optional)

MAKES 4 SERVINGS

Per serving:
103 calories
2 g protein
2 g fat (0.3 g sat)
25 g carbohydrates
10 mg sodium
32 mg calcium
2 g fiber

Put the milk and cocoa powder in a medium saucepan and whisk until the cocoa powder is completely dissolved and no lumps remain. Add the water, sugar, and chile and bring to a boil over medium-high heat, stirring almost constantly. Decrease the heat to low and simmer gently, stirring frequently, for 5 minutes. Add the creamer, optional cinnamon, and optional vanilla extract and stir until well combined. Remove from the heat, remove the chile, and serve immediately.

Comradery Corn

After dinner, the crew often gathers in the mess to watch a movie or play games. And because popcorn is central to our comradery, this snack is a staple in our diets. Over time, I've decided that the best way to make popcorn is on the stove top.

3 tablespoons (45 ml) vegetable oil
½ cup (125 ml) popping corn kernels
Salt (optional)
Sugar (optional)

Heat the oil in a medium soup pot over medium-high heat until it just starts to smoke, about 1 minute. Add the kernels and cover with a tight-fitting lid. When you hear the first few pops, after about 1 minute, shake the pot over the heat to prevent the kernels from burning. Continue to shake the pot as the kernels pop. When most of the kernels have popped, crack the lid so the popped corn doesn't become soggy. When the popping has stopped, after 3 to 4 minutes, immediately remove from the heat. Pour into a large serving bowl. Season to taste with salt or sugar or both if desired.

MAKES 12 CUPS (3 L) OF POPPED CORN

Per 1 cup:
37 calories
0 g protein
4 g fat (1 g sat)
1 g carbohydrates
1 mg sodium
0 mg calcium
0 g fiber

Note: Analysis does not include optional salt or sugar.

HEADING HOME

This is the single most wonderful sentence that the Sea Shepherd crew hears during the course of a campaign:

"The whaling fleet has abandoned the slaughter, and we are free to return home!"

Because of Sea Shepherd's relentless pursuit of the fleet, we've been able to fully shut down the whalers and send them running home for several consecutive years. Fortified with the knowledge that the Antarctic whales are safe, at least until next year, we also turn and head for port. With this victory behind us, we look forward to enjoying the company of our families and friends, whom we have missed over Christmas and who have supported us without fail.

Every year, I find the campaign crew to be a collection of interesting, compassionate, and dedicated people. It's such a pleasure and privilege to spend time with individuals who are willing to give up their comforts and work damn hard helping to end the disgusting slaughter of whales.

As we head for home, emotions run wild beneath a calm surface. The crew's morale is in a weird place as we prepare for the final leg of the campaign. We're still buzzing from the many long weeks of action against the whaling fleet. Yet our exhilaration is tempered by the exhaustion that comes from the seven months of nonstop work that goes into preparing the ship and then taking it on campaign.

The days at sea take their toll on your entire being, both physically and emotionally. You're continuously subject to the steady droning of engines; the sometimes violent rolling, corkscrewing, and pitching movement of the ship; the subtle mechanical vibration that hums relentlessly through your body. Then the moment comes to pull in alongside, and quite suddenly, everything is silent and still.

Briefly, as we arrive in port, I feel a pull to be back underway. Then my body remembers what it's like to have two feet planted firmly on the ground, and I'm overcome by a desire to jump onto the dock. My first impulse is to run to the first nonhuman being I can find and hug it. This is followed closely by a yen for fresh fruit and vegetables—a feast, accompanied by a cold beer.

Yes, I welcome the comforts of land. But I treasure the gifts of the sea. I've had the pleasure of hanging out with whales during many Antarctic summers. I've seen them play and dive, run and scream, and die. Being on campaign is an emotional roller coaster, and I've had experiences in Antarctica that I neither want to remember nor forget.

Each year we aim to cause sufficient economic damage to the whaling fleet so they can never return to Antarctica. But if we can't permanently cripple them, we'll return and continue to fight. We will never back down, until they stop the killing.

ACKNOWLEDGMENTS

First, I'd like to thank all the awesome folks who have come through the Sea Shepherd galleys over the past decade and helped me learn how to cook, particularly Krissie, Birdy, Raffa, Vera, and Merrilee. The galleys are such wonderful places to learn, and everyone is welcome to come in and teach us their favorite dishes.

Thanks to the people who contributed recipes: Paul, Merrilee, Ronnie, Jo, Mal, and Vera.

Thank you to Paul Watson and Sea Shepherd for providing a platform for the most amazing learning adventures. All crew members have the opportunity while on board to learn endless skills, many of which set us off on wonderful lifelong journeys.

And finally, thanks to all my friends and family who have lent me their kitchens to cook in—and their bellies to experiment on!

Remember that revolution can begin in the kitchen—spread the food love!

INDEX

BookPublishing Co.

books that educate, inspire, and empower

To find your favorite books on plant-based cooking and nutrition,
living foods lifestyle, and healthy living, visit:
BookPubCo.com

Artisan Vegan Cheese

Miyoko Schinner

978-1-57067-283-5 • $19.95

Leff Love

Kittee Berns

978-1-57067-311-5 • $19.95

Cookin' Crunk

Bianca Phillips

978-1-57067-268-2 • $19.95

Eat Vegan on $4 a Day

Ellen Jaffe Jones

978-1-57067-257-6 • $14.95

**Becoming Vegan:
Express Edition**

*Brenda Davis, RD,
Vesanto Melina, MS, RD*

978-1-57067-295-8 • $19.95

Bravo!

Chef Ramses Bravo

978-1-57067-269-9 • $19.95

Purchase these health titles and cookbooks from your local bookstore or natural food store,
or you can buy them directly from:

Book Publishing Company • P.O. Box 99 • Summertown, TN 38483 • 1-888-260-8458

Please include $3.95 per book for shipping and handling.